P9-CJJ-406

Journeys Through the Garden

Inspiration for Gardeners in B.C. and the Pacific Northwest

Journeys Through the Garden

Inspiration for Gardeners in B.C. and the Pacific Northwest

Paddy Wales

Whitecap Books
Vancouver / Toronto

Whitecap Books
Vancouver/Toronto

Edited by Elaine Jones
Proofread by Elizabeth McLean
Cover and interior photos by Paddy Wales
Cover design by Tanya Lloyd
Interior design by Tanya Lloyd

Printed and bound in Canada

Canadian Cataloguing in Publication Data

Wales, Paddy, 1951–
Journeys through the garden

Includes index.
ISBN 1-55110-786-4

1. Gardening—British Columbia. 2. Gardening—Northwest, Pacific. 3. Gardens—British Columbia. 4. Gardens—Northwest, Pacific. I. Title.
SB453.3.C2W23 1998 635.9'09711 C98-910660-8

The publisher acknowledges the support of the Canada Council and the Cultural Services Branch of the Government of British Columbia in making this publication possible. We acknowledge the financial support of the Government of Canada through the Book Publishing Industry Development Program for our publishing activities.

acknowledgments

I am deeply indebted to Nancy Webber, midwife to this book, whose insights, encouragement, and assistance at photo shoots were invaluable. My first manuscript readers, Nancy, Donna Welstein, Kathy Leishman, and Geri Barnes, gave substantial suggestions and technical advice, as well as confidence to complete the project. Marjorie Harris's words of introduction are too generous.

A thousand thanks go to the gardeners who inspired me. Their gardening experiences shaped this book. They welcomed me into their gardens, and some of these magical places appear in the photographs. I am indebted to Cliff and Rosemary Bailey, Geri Barnes, Robert and Birgit Bateman, Brent Beattie, Susanna Blunt, Joan and Joel Brink, Patricia Burgess, Ken and Eileen Cambon, Elisabeth and Peter Carey, Eleanor Carnwath, Margaret Charlton, Terri Clark, Marion Clarke, Elaine Corbet, Marianne Côté-Malley, Therese d'Monte, Margaret and Paul Daniels, Francisca Darts, Ellen and Jan deMan, Trudy and Ian Dixon, Louise Dyer, Elizabeth England, Doris Fancourt-Smith, Nori Fletcher, Barbara Flynn, Pamela Frost, Linda Gravelin, Shirley Hebenton, Dan Hinkley, Thomas Hobbs, Sandra Holloway, Jocelyn Horder, Dan Jason, Jennifer Jones, Kathy Leishman, Bob Lilly, Audrey Litherland, Elizabeth Litherland, Michael Luco, Maureen Lunn, Barbara and Peter Mason, Valerie Murray, Judy Newton, Lyn Noble, Phoebe Noble, Audrey Ostrom, Calvor Palmateer, Glen Patterson, Brenda Peterson, Valerie Pfeiffer, Clare Philips, Kathy Poole, Ken and Theresa Rowley, Susan Ryley, Charles Sale, Brenda Scherbatty, Elaine Stevens, Mary Stewart, Richard Stewart, Basil Stuart-Stubbs, David Tarrant, Karin and Heinz Tigges, Olga Towert, Nancy Webber, Stuart Webber, Terry Welch, and Claire and Jamie Wright; and to these businesses and public gardens: Bellevue Botanical Garden, Everlasting Summer, Heronswood Nursery, Hollyhock Farm, Park and Tilford Gardens, University of British Columbia Botanical Garden, and VanDusen Botanical Garden.

contents

foreword

My first meeting with Paddy Wales was at a gathering of gardeners. I had come west to give a talk as part of a Philosophy of Gardening seminar. At the end of the day, Glen Patterson took me aside to show me some slides of his garden. What amazing photographs, I thought. The photographer had absolutely caught the spirit of his glorious garden.

When I was introduced to her later that evening, it was one of those immediate moments of warmth. I found Paddy's freshness and enthusiasm appealing and her tart sense of humor right up my alley. When I connected this person with the photographs I'd seen earlier in the day, I was thrilled. Here was a photographer who not only gardens but also knows what that weird-looking plant is reflected in the lens.

So, for many years, I thought of her as Paddy, the photographer. We started corresponding, comparing our east and west gardening experiences. I found her insights entertaining, useful, and funny. I watched as she emerged as a serious writer.

Her articles appeared in Canadian gardening magazines at about the same time her photographs were beginning to be published in American magazines. She managed to winkle out the best from the gardeners she interviewed as well as taking shots of the gardens always at their peak. I've been with her on location shooting: she has the profound patience needed in waiting for the light, as well as a persistent curiosity about each plant she focuses on.

Journeys Through the Garden is an eloquent testament to a passion for photography, writing, and gardening. For those of us who don't live in the Pacific Northwest, a certain amount of garden envy is naturally going to bubble to the surface. Nevertheless, Paddy has got it just right. This book will enchant not only regional gardeners, but anyone who has a love of gardening.

—*Marjorie Harris*

Inspiration

Like our cities, homes, and institutions, the gardening tradition here on the west coast of Canada and the Pacific Northwest states is new. Our styles are emergent, a fusion of traditions from other homelands with this extraordinary land.

I was raised on the prairies and in Ontario, and carry with me two childhood landscapes—the golden vastness of Saskatchewan and the dark greens of boreal woodlands. The experience of being shorter than the field grasses, making a house by stomping them flat, and lying low out of view of parents is a special memory that still affects my notion of *garden.* So does the recollection of scampering along a forest path, not paved or flat, but twisting over tree roots and around rocks.

The west coast landscape exerts huge impact on our psyches. Those raised here do not always appreciate the weight of winter's rains on newcomers, or credit how ready access to wilderness fires the imagination. Like many gardeners here, my original understanding of *landscape* has been overwritten by the sheer might of this terrain—seemingly endless mountains, a forest of trees that, even in second growth, dwarf us with their enormity and inspire us with their elegance. The rocky seashores, the scent of salt on the air, and the rain, rain, rain mold us as surely as we mold the land on which we garden.

The meeting of mountains and ocean is not only the order of our land, but also the crux of our climate. The steady onslaught of winter storm systems

OPPOSITE:
Near the author's home in West Vancouver, B.C., a blast of northern outflow wind meets the Coast Mountains and the moderating waters of Georgia Strait.

ABOVE:
Part of painter Robert Bateman's garden is inspired by west coast rain forest, a cool, moist oasis in the often dry Gulf Island landscape. Native sword ferns (*Polystichum munitum*) and deer ferns (*Blechnum spicant*) thrive here.

In a partially shady segment of Karin and Heinz Tigges' garden, a lichen-encrusted rock is an elegant, ancient object and a textural contrast to leaves of *Helleborus argutifolius* and *Primula japonica.*

(about a hundred a year!), cold and wet from the Gulf of Alaska or warm and wet from Hawaii, is the secret to the remarkable winter cloak of evergreen we enjoy. When freezing, desiccating Arctic air flows through the mountain passes and ocean inlets, we have a shuddering reminder (and perhaps a smidgen of smugness) of what winter might be like elsewhere.

The Arctic air is a limiting factor for what plants we may grow. If for most of the year we have only mild frost, the few weeks of bitter weather prevent us from keeping tender plants unprotected out of doors. Overnight temperatures that suddenly plummet, daytime thawing sunshine, and drying winds are a combination lethal to some plants. When a storm off the ocean collides with the cold, the resulting snow is usually heavy and wet. In other northern areas of the continent, people arm themselves with snow blowers; we use brooms and rakes to release our bamboo and rhododendrons from oppressive blobs of snow. We cannot count on all-winter snow to insulate the roots of plants, but most years we experience its oppressive weight and its sudden enchantment.

High winter rainfall is the other factor that guides our choices of plants. If our soil is not well enough drained, plants that easily withstand cold may perish from roots rotted in winter and spring. Where soil drains freely, even the Mediterranean and desert plants adapted for drought survive, waiting all winter for their chance to dry out and perform in summer. We experience drought conditions for part of each summer when watering restrictions apply in many areas.

Our soil is generally acidic, a result of the high rainfall. Although there are spotty exceptions where alkaline conditions exist, most of us may choose acid-tolerant plants, such as heather, blueberry, or rhododendron, without worry. Those plants requiring neutral or alkaline soil need a continuing program of soil amendment (usually with dolomite lime) to lower the acidity. Luckily, many plants accept a wide range of soil alkalinity, provided the soil

Climate zones

Many growers and garden writers refer to the zone of a plant. Zones are a way of predicting whether a plant will survive in the climate conditions of a region. There are several different zone systems in use, but the one most commonly found is the United States Department of Agriculture (USDA) system based on the average minimum temperatures in winter. The Pacific Northwest has zones ranging from 7 through 9. The system is unquestionably helpful in selecting plants, and it is a good idea to know your approximate zone by asking at local garden centers or master gardener clinics. However, this information cannot tell you which plants will survive because it ignores such factors as summer temperatures, wind, rainfall, snow cover, or drainage. Within one community, even within one garden, there are areas that are moister and drier, more exposed to winter winds, or more prone to frost.

Adventuresome gardeners like to cheat the weather. They push the limits of their zone with plants that are reputedly too tender. They enjoy the challenge of protecting these plants in winter, and providing the optimal soil and drainage conditions to give their special plants a fighting chance. Playful terms such as zonophobes (I'm afraid to try anything iffy), zone denial (if a plant doesn't survive in someone else's garden, surely it will in mine), and zone cowboys (I don't care what anybody says, I'm growing that plant) are all part of the fun.

texture—moisture retentive but well drained is the easiest to work with, but rarely what we are given—is suitable.

There is much talk about changing climate, and gardeners will have to pay attention. It remains to be seen whether we find ourselves with a wetter, milder, northern Californian climate, or a harsher climate that is colder in winter and hotter in summer. One gardener I know recently planted a coast redwood (*Sequoia sempervirens*) in anticipation of change that may occur over the next decades. Another is gaining experience with a wider range of crops by trying out vegetable seeds not traditionally grown in the coastal climate and sowing earlier in spring and later in fall than before.

One thing is sure: gardens are not static. It helps if we see our gardens as places in flux. Every garden photograph is out of date by the time it is developed, a record of how things were. Neither are gardeners ever fully formed, ever fully finished.

Gardening is an expression of desire. We yearn for beauty, for sensual stimulation, for an experience of the elemental. Each time we dig, turn, rake, weed, sow, plant, mulch, we regain a connection with the earth, re-attain,

Time to winterize

To take the bite out of winter, here are steps you can take to prevent plants dying from freezing, desiccation, or rotting roots. Most hardy plants will survive unattended, but if your garden experiences especially strong Arctic winds, a few will need help.

- Use mulch on top of the soil to keep the soil temperature from dropping or rising too suddenly. An eight-inch (twenty-centimetre) layer of mulch will prevent roots of such borderline-hardy plants as agapanthus from freezing. Remove this mulch in spring.
- Place fallen evergreen boughs or dead fern fronds over plants that may not like cold.
- Protect plants in pots by grouping them together, preferably somewhere out of the wind, keeping them under an overhang to prevent waterlogging, and using boughs around and on top of the pots themselves.
- In exposed gardens, keep on hand a stack of burlap sacks, old beach towels, or even heavy plastic. When the temperature is predicted to stay well below freezing, wrap the most vulnerable shrubs.
- To prevent rot in plants that prefer drought, make a lean-to over the plant's crown with tempered glass or hard clear plastic.

In making his garden, Richard Stewart had no earth at all with which to work; his garden is on a rooftop. He has planted trees in containers, clumps of bamboo, grasses, groundcovers, and dwarf conifers, all in containers. The mostly monochromatic green and variegated plants are cool and inviting in the urban setting. Dozens of glazed ceramic pots, several small cement tables, and a large Thai peace-bell add an exotic flavor.

Richard has emphasized plants with contrasting forms and textures, Asian and west coast influences to make a stroll along the length of the garden a rich experience.

for a time, part of our natural selves. In this era gardening has great potential as a positive force if, as is increasingly the case, we touch the soil with care, demonstrating our wish for an environment that is as healthy as it is beautiful.

Over the past years I have struggled to make two gardens, one in the thin, dry, shaded soil beneath tall conifers in West Vancouver, B.C., the other on the sunny, windswept, salt-soaked beach at Robert's Creek, northwest of

Homemade furniture such as Cliff Bailey's whimsical bench adds humor as well as function.

Vancouver. My gardens have been strongly influenced by the many local gardeners who have shared with me what they grow and how they work. Sometimes they have told me the sources of their inspiration—trips to famous gardens in Europe or Japan, books by eminent horticulturists, wilderness hikes, gardening courses and lectures, guidance from older gardeners.

Gardeners with more knowledge, more experience, and more courage have helped me tremendously. By walking slowly through their gardens, looking hard at what they have created (in some cases despite severe obstacles of steep terrain, cramped spaces, tiny budgets, or uncooperative mates), and by listening to their stories, I have begun to imagine greater gardens.

There is no substitute for visiting gardens, and every garden offers a useful lesson or two. While we may be tempted to take more photographs and buy more souvenir books of grand gardens in England or California, even modest local gardens may offer better insight into what is possible here. One summer, four neighbors and I walked along our street to peek into our gardens, none visible from the road. We talked about the rocky outcroppings, the dry shade, finding the protected areas for more tender plants and coping with the spots vulnerable to the bitter winter winds that flow out of Burrard Inlet. The exchange of information was specific and invaluable.

Inspiration is important, but sometimes I am overwhelmed by the ravishing gardens on tours. Mine seems crude by comparison. However, frustration is one of the best motivations for change in any area of life. To find the courage necessary to follow our own garden dreams, we need to come home to what we have, who we are, and what we want. We all have biases about building materials, plants, shapes, moods, styles. I love licheny rocks, mossy paths, rounded beach stones, and sun-bleached cedar boards. I also admire brick, gravel, wrought iron, and concrete used well in other gardens,

Improve your drainage

Water-loving bog plants can make a beautiful display, but most other plants hate having their roots sit in water. Improving your drainage widens the choice of plants that will thrive. Water tends to collect at the base of a hill and in dips in the contour of the land.

- Mound up planting areas by adding soil and such organic material as leaf mold, well-rotted compost or manure.
- For plants that need sharp drainage, add grit or rock chips to soil. Make raised beds edged with rock or wood.
- To heavy clay soil, add sand and plenty of organic material. Deep digging will break up the clay immediately, but eventually the sand will work its way down to do the job with less effort.
- Add a drainage system such as a soakway (a water collection pit filled with chunks of concrete and rock, topped with gravel and soil) or a gravel-filled ditch – or build a complete system of buried drainage tile or plastic drain tubing to remove standing water.

but I do not covet them. Ferns, clematis, euphorbias, and ornamental grasses speak to me more than toad lilies, photinias, lavender, or lawn. Of course, these preferences may change radically over time (I'm rethinking the toad lilies), but admitting my partiality helps define what I should do next.

Budget, for many, is a significant constraint, especially when considering structures that require purchased materials and skilled labor. It may be small comfort that money alone cannot make a wonderful garden, but the fact that many exquisite gardens have been made inexpensively gives me heart. Low walls may be built with found rocks, paths made with bark mulch instead of pavers, trellises fashioned from prunings. There are excellent courses that teach skills in masonry and carpentry. Labor may be traded between neighbors—construction of an arbor in exchange for baby-sitting.

The budget can easily be blown on plants purchased whenever the car swerves into the garden center parking lot. A seasonal plan helps, even if you do not follow it to the letter. Trees and large shrubs warrant careful research.

A garden journal

Some people are natural diarists, recording the daily weather, the progress of plants, birds spotted, tasks completed, successes and failures of the season, and plans for next year. Far more common are the would-be garden journalists — those who start the year with eloquent notes about the garden in January, with good intentions to continue all year. Too soon comes the choice: should I go out in the garden and dig, or just write about it?

Commercially produced journals may be very attractive and have enough cues and reminders to spur the reluctant record-keeper to write regularly. A photo album is a good chronicle, especially for showing how the garden changes over the years. Some gardeners keep a guest book; after all, visitors and their comments are important. A spiral notebook, an accordion file, even a large manila envelope can serve to hold plant labels, lecture notes, and sketches of where the bulbs were planted. Record the date on anything worth keeping — plant labels, seed packets, sketches, plans. Use a china marker or soft pencil to mark a label of a new plant with the month and year it was purchased. To write more easily on a photo, affix a mailing label to the back. If you are unlikely to keep an orderly record, at least put all the notes in one place. (I toss all labels into a bathroom drawer.)

The point of keeping all this information is that it is helpful later. If a climbing rose turns out to be the

Valerie Pfeiffer grows a lively palette of flowers, a stimulus for her watercolor paintings. Favorite subjects include trailing perennial sweet pea (*Lathyrus latifolius*), scarlet bee balm (*Monarda didyma*), California poppies (*Eschscholzia californica*), and annual cosmos (*Cosmos bipinnatus*).

envy of the neighbors, it is a shame to admit you don't know what it is. If expensive bulbs fail to perform, it's foolish to repeat the mistake. And every time you feel the gruesome slice of the spade through a lily bulb, you'll wish you'd had a planting diagram to consult.

A garden journal is entertaining to review, regardless of whether it is a thorough archive or a jumble of snapshots and scraps of paper. Many serious gardeners though, especially plant collectors, develop a system to list their plants and cross-reference with garden diagrams. Each area of the garden has a name — perhaps its location (Front West), a significant plant in the area (Parrotia Bed), or the growing condition (The Bog). Those who grow plants from seeds need to record information about the seed source and dates planted and germinated.

More and more, these records are kept on computers for accuracy and ease of update. For most people, sketches of proposed design changes are easier with a pencil than with a computer mouse, but design software can be both useful and fun.

One of the advantages of sketching in the garden is that it necessitates close observation. Through history, and no less today, botanists and gardeners have made pencil drawings of everything from seeds in their pods to entire garden landscapes. This is not just record-keeping, it is a way of looking.

Where will they be planted? How will they grow over the next decades? Attractive, healthy trees suitable to the garden are a worthy investment. Scrimp on annuals. Increase your stock of perennials by taking cuttings or making plant divisions. Find plant trading partners on the block, in the family, at work. Buy a few packets of seed and learn how to grow choice plants for next to nothing. Frugality and cleverness have always been valued among gardeners.

Few of our gardens slip easily into a single style. Perhaps because we have so many influences from cultures around the world, we rarely follow one approach to the exclusion of others. It might be simpler to adopt a formula for an instant Japanese or English cottage garden, but a reproduction tends to become an imitation. A satisfying style is a personal one that seeks many influences, but chooses carefully which will carry weight.

Gardens fit into our lives in such highly personal ways. The gourmet cook wants the freshest herbs and vegetables. The painter seeks color and form. The carpenter likes to add wooden planters, decks, gazebos. The children want a soccer pitch; their parents need a retreat. One gardener I know is only happy when he can change the landscape in big ways, making hillside terraces for grape vines, planting fruit trees by fives and tens, throwing

Looking at gardens

In June and July, many of us take advantage of the tours of private gardens sponsored by garden clubs and community groups. To make the most of these opportunities:

- Take one photo that shows the overall site, then concentrate on smaller vignettes that show how a few plants are well put together.
- Choose your favorite segment of the garden, then imagine it in all four seasons.
- Talk to the garden's owner about specifics. Tell what you like, and ask what the most difficult tasks have been.
- Be selective about which plants you identify, and record their names accurately. Most of us can learn only a few new plant names in a day. Carry a good reference book in your car.
- Pick the most critical spots for viewing the garden (from the front door step, or from the top of a path) to see how the design works.
- Show genuine interest in the intentions of the gardener as well as the accomplishments. You just may meet a lifelong gardening friend.

Valerie Murray's house and garden show her love of experimentation with color, form, and texture and her fascination with unusual plants.

up sturdy sheds, lifting huge boulders for rock walls. Another works the land more delicately, handling each bulb, flower, tree, and vigorous groundcover with reverence. We all want beautiful surroundings and healthy gardens; the ways we go about it are diverse.

At times I feel my garden is awkward, messy, graceless, and without hope. I am embarrassed to let anyone see it until it is completely renovated. However, some of my best jumps forward have been the result of friends who visit, say kind things, then give suggestions. I rarely follow their advice literally, but I am struck by their insights, and mull their comments over and over. When a visitor comes, I feel my eyes are seeing the garden anew. Things I have learned to ignore—the heap of pruned branches awaiting disposal, the unfinished path, the house next door—are suddenly very obvious. I realize

In a dry, sunny part of her garden, Kathy Leishman has allowed self-seeding plants to set a joyful, carefree tone. Annuals, such as field poppies (*Papaver rhoeas*) and rocket candytuft (*Iberis amara*), and biennials such as foxgloves (*Digitalis purpurea*) and blue bugloss (*Echium vulgare*) are well established, appearing in new combinations each spring.

I have concentrated too much on the little things, dear trilliums and violets, and have forgotten to shape the garden with shrubs and trees. Now I am charged with the excitement of possibility. I know what I need to learn, and can take the next step. Let the play begin.

Home weddings, impending garden club visits, and reunions are events that may impel us to prune back the branches encroaching on the sidewalk, plant a little more lavishly, and make an obsession of tidying. Changes that will increase our year-round enjoyment of the garden and carry more personal meaning take longer, and the motivation must be found within. Photographs of the garden bolster me greatly. Few people think to take "before" pictures, but in truth, any time is before the future. It gives me courage to see that the garden has changed for the better in the past few years, and I cherish the old dreary pictures that prove it. I take pictures from above looking down, from the entrance gate looking in, and from where I like to sit looking all around. I try to remember to take photographs in fall and winter, not just when flowers are out. Few of these images are ones I show other people; they are useful to me, and not brag-shots to pass round. I take those too, but more selectively, showing only vignettes of the segments of the garden with which I am, for now, satisfied.

There are gardeners who draw detailed plans to scale on huge sheets of graph paper, revising a dozen times before work commences. For these people, I have great admiration. I cannot work this way. My best ideas have been flashes, acted on impulsively, then refined in the doing. Unfortunately, so have my worst ideas. But like climate, site, and budget, the gardener's quirks are givens, at once constraints and opportunities.

Our gardens evoke a mood—rugged or romantic, sensual or cerebral, contemplative or jolly. The garden's layout, its structures and the materials used, its openness or enclosure, the trees and large plants, the inclusion of water or rock, all contribute to ambience. So do the more personal details—the furniture and containers, smaller plants, treasured objects. Noting how elements in other people's gardens contribute to mood helps clarify the character of our own gardens, and indicates ways it may be reinforced.

As we take our individual garden journeys, illuminated by images of those singular gardens that could belong to no one but their owners and exist on no other site, we make our own gardens authentic by pleasing ourselves.

Natural Elements

The window above my desk overlooks a trio of Douglas fir trunks, two massive ones with a slender intermediary, all set off by the rich green scales of a cedar behind. The firs and western hemlocks, some eighty years old, and western red cedars, younger yet similarly sized, cast a year-round shadow, but also protect from fall or late spring frosts. The licheny gray-green trunks of the Doug firs give me special pleasure; their weighty vertical architecture could never be duplicated by manufactured materials. They are the *genius loci* of this garden, the spirit of place that guides and inspires, limits and opens opportunities for expressing my sense of *here*. They comfort, uplift, distract; nuthatches, flickers, and woodpeckers explore their trunks; the changing light transforms them from severe pillars to velvety paint strokes. I feel lucky, and humbled, to be in their presence; they were here before I was born, and will likely be here when I am gone.

Natural gardening has come to mean several different things. To one it may mean cultivating native plants; to another, using nature as the inspiration for a naturalistic design or employing indigenous building materials; to yet another it means attracting birds and other wildlife to the garden. It may even mean disturbing nature's garden as little as possible. But the essence of natural gardening is careful observation of nature. By watching the ways climate and terrain shape our landscapes and learning how our native plants and animals are adapted to their homes, we are best able to interpret our desire for natural gardens in our own ways.

Opposite:
Beneath Douglas firs (*Pseudotsuga menziesii*) in the author's garden, Korean dogwood (*Cornus kousa*) glistens and black bamboo (*Phyllostachys nigra*) arches over in autumn rain.

Above:
Skunk cabbage (*Lysichiton americanus*) is a desirable west coast native.

It is our good fortune to have some native plants coveted by gardeners around the world. Our humbly named skunk cabbage (*Lysichiton americanus*), for instance, is sold by the most prestigious nurseries in England, where its common name is swamp lantern. In the wild here it thrives on wet slopes, along stream margins and in boggy areas, its promising yellow flower shoots emerging shyly in earliest spring, their huge spathes opening dramatically, followed by handsome broad leaves. Although its near relative *L. camtschatcensis,* which has a white spathe, is native to Japan, some Japanese gardeners are desperate to grow our yellow skunk cabbage.

Our common native plants—salal and Oregon grape; Douglas fir, western red cedar, and western hemlock; even our graceful vine maple, arbutus, and Garry oak—are often overlooked as garden plants just because they are common. It is absurd that we need the validation of plant collectors and horticulturists elsewhere in the world to begin to cherish the familiar plants that grow so well for us.

This is changing rapidly. We have an increasing number of superb small nurseries specializing in native plants grown from seed or propagated from nursery stock. Where once choice plants such as trilliums, erythroniums, or camas were plucked from the wild to satisfy the demand from connoisseurs, now the purchase of these plants need not diminish wild stocks. But the situation is not completely rosy, and the caveat Buyer Beware is as advisable now as ever. With the burgeoning demand for native species, some plant sellers still buy stock stripped from the wild. Two rules of thumb apply: always ask the source of native plants, and be suspicious of bargains. The same scruples apply to individual gardeners—it is simply wrong to dig plants from the wild to use in the garden. Savvy gardeners, however, look for opportunities to save plants from house demolitions, areas about to be cleared for new subdivisions, or road construction.

For years I had looked longingly at the vine maple saplings along the edge of a gravel lane leading into my neighborhood park. I was sorely tempted to bring home one or two but was saved from sin partly by procrastination and partly from fear of severing their roots and killing the young trees.

Hosta fortunei var. *albopicta*, *Primula japonica*, *Saxifraga* × *urbium* create a textured floor in Geri Barnes' garden.

Like many plant aficionados, garden designer Geri Barnes has a keen interest in plants as individual specimens, valued in her case especially for their leaves and growth habits. Her serene woodland garden works as a unified three-dimensional space, rather than as a display or collection. Although it is a small suburban garden, it is layered like a forest. Beneath the high canopy of several native conifers, small deciduous trees and large rhododendrons form masses and openings like clearings in the woods at and above eye level. A wealth of smaller flowering shrubs and perennials grows below them, and at ankle height, tiny ground-hugging treasures and lacy groundcovers abound.

A walk through this layered garden is full of thoughtful pauses. Look ahead at a flurry of electric blue-mauve *Rhododendron augustinii* trusses. Catch the reflection of light on a cement urn used as a water vessel. It is a highly crafted design where Geri's attention to unity and rhythm, variety and repetition, light and shadow, complementary and contrasting textures give the garden its naturalism.

nature by design

The day a backhoe began to excavate for a new electrical line, I asked the foreman where he planned to dig, and ran for a shovel to rescue two knee-high maples in the line of destruction. These have survived, one in my garden and the other in a neighbor's, only half a block from their original home. It was a very minor act of conservation, but the principle of preserving our plant heritage and diversity on private lands is increasingly important in this era of rapid population growth and habitat devastation.

Like the word natural, *native* sometimes appears in catalog plant descriptions without specifying exactly where in the world the plant is native. "Native to North America" is just too general to be useful. (Not many plants from the Florida everglades would be suitable anywhere else on the continent!) "Native to the Pacific Northwest" is a much more useful descriptor, although each plant from the region has its own habitat preferences. Most of the plants native to northeastern North America will also thrive here. One very strict interpretation of *native gardening* is using only plants originating within fifty miles (eighty kilometres) of the garden in question. I do not consider this a more

Northwest natives to know and grow

- *Adiantum pedatum* (maidenhair fern). Forms a handsome clump of lacy fronds on knee-high shiny blue-black stems; deciduous. Moist shade to part shade.
- *Ceanothus impressus* 'Victoria' (California lilac). Small-leafed evergreen shrub with dark blue flowers. Full sun, well-drained soil, protected site.
- *Erythronium tuolumnense* (yellow fawn lily). An exquisite erythronium worth growing for angelic flowers and broad mottled leaves. Rich woodland soil, part shade.
- *Ribes sanguineum* (flowering currant). Deciduous shrub with panicles of deep rose flowers. Sun to part shade, well-drained soil. 'White Icicle' is a choice white variety. Many other native currants are available; all draw hummingbirds.
- *Garrya elliptica* (silk tassel bush). Evergreen with leathery leaves and long slinky catkins in winter. For berries, a male and female are needed. 'James Roof' and 'Evie' are available cultivars with very long tassels; *G.* × *issaquahensis* 'Pat Ballard' is more upright. Sun to part shade, well-drained soil.
- *Gymnocarpium dryopteris* (oak fern). Low deciduous fern forming a lacy mat by underground rhizomes. Shade.
- *Polystichum munitum* (sword fern). Evergreen fern forming a large

Large-leafed hostas combine well with the delicate forms of maidenhair fern in Geri Barnes' shade garden.

mound. Once established, can be left unattended or cropped back in late winter. Sun to shade, dry to moist (how agreeable!).

- *Tolmiea menziesii* (piggyback plant), so called because its leaves have buds that root when they touch the soil and form daughter plants. Evergreen perennial; the variegated form is very pretty. Part to full shade.
- *Trillium ovatum* (western trillium). Perennial growing from a thick rhizome; brilliant white flowers fade to pink and maroon. Well-drained, leafy soil; part shade.
- *Vancouveria hexandra.* Deciduous groundcover bearing small white flowers in late spring; its leaves are similar to but more finely textured than its relatives, the epimediums. Part shade.
- And there are many more wonderful native plants to discover: *Arctostaphylos uva-ursi* (kinnikinnik), *Camassia* (camas lily), *Calochortus* species (fairy lanterns), *Dodecatheon* species (shooting star), *Gaultheria shallon* (salal), *Lysichiton americanus* (skunk cabbage), *Mahonia aquifolium* (Oregon grape), *Dicentra formosa* (western bleeding heart), *Iris tenax* (Oregon iris), *Rosa nutkana* (Nootka rose), *Symphoricarpos albus* (snowberry), *Viburnum trilobum* (highbush cranberry).

Glen Patterson's pond and bridge evoke nature's own artistry, shown here in winter.

natural or superior way of gardening, but it is an interesting exercise in local plant knowledge.

Wild, usually referring to wildflowers, refers to any plant that grows in the wild. This includes a great many garden escapees, such as purple foxglove (*Digitalis purpurea*) and rose campion (*Lychnis coronaria*), both European natives. Their freely seeding habit of popping up unbidden and untended makes them alternately a welcome wildflower or a despised weed.

To most gardeners the terminology is less important than the plants. A naturalistic garden is one where the plants are so well suited to their specific sites and grown in combinations of such natural grace, they give the impression of growing naturally. Often these plants need less care to thrive once they become established because they originate from a climate similar to ours. In fact, some of the most exciting plants used in naturalistic gardens are, like many of us, newcomers from elsewhere in the world.

Plant hunters such as Dan Hinkley of Heronswood Nursery in Kingston, Washington, are mounting expeditions to Asia and South America, especially the mountainous regions of Chile, China, Japan, Korea, and the Himalayas, in a renaissance of seed collection that parallels the great plant explorations of past centuries. Fueled in part by the currently hot horticultural market, and by the new opportunities for travel to areas previously closed to Westerners, these expeditions are funded by private subscribers, botanical gardens, and such organizations as the Royal Horticultural Society, the American Rhododendron Society, and the venerable Alpine Garden Club

When you wore a *Tulipa*

The terminology and Latin of plant names can be frustrating, even maddening. The purpose of botanical Latin is clarity, not confusion. For instance, dozens of gray-leafed plants are known and sold as dusty miller. If you want *Helichrysum petiolare,* you may not be happy to substitute *Senecio cineraria, Lychnis coronaria,* or *Artemisia stellerana,* all also known as dusty miller. Common names vary from region to region. What Americans call a madrona tree, Canadians call an arbutus.

Once you begin to learn a few of the patterns of botanical Latin and recognize some of the vocabulary, you may actually like it. Some like it so much they abandon English altogether, using *Tulipa* where tulip would do nicely. And just when you've mastered a few of the names, get ready for the news that the botanists have reorganized, reclassified, or otherwise renamed your favorites. For clarity.

Here are a few of the taxonomic basics. Each plant belongs to a group called a genus (plural, *genera*). A genus may have many *species* within it. These two parts of the name are always in Latin, and printed in italics. As the Latin word for maple is *Acer,* all the maples' names begin with the same word, *Acer.* Our native species, the big-leaf maple, is *Acer macrophyllum,* from *macro,* big, and *phyllum,* leaf. Sometimes a species is named for a botanist (*Acer davidii*) or a region (*Acer pennsylvaticum*), rather than a description of the plant. Many of the Japanese maples are *Acer palmatum,* or hand-like maples, but among these are distinct variations. For instance, there are lacy or dissected leaves, red leaves, red lacy leaves, or extremely lacy leaves. Once a unique variant is selected for use in our gardens, it is referred to as a cultivar (cultivated variety). Cultivars have their names in single quotes without italics, such as *Acer palmatum* 'Garnet'.

Then there are the rules of grammatical agreement, arguments about whether two names refer to the same plant, the vagaries of pronunciation, and recently, trademarks. But don't be put off, it's all in the name of clarity, and it's a little like a secret handshake among gardeners.

of British Columbia. Seeds collected are made available to sponsoring subscribers around the world. If successfully germinated, these new-to-horticulture plants appear first in the gardens of scientists and serious collectors, who raise them and share cuttings or seeds with others in the horticultural hierarchy. If reasonably easy to propagate, they may find their way to specialized plant sales and then into the nursery trade. The first generations of plants newly introduced to commerce may be frightfully expensive, giving them a cachet of irresistibility. The most successful from the point of view of beauty, garden vigor, and ease of propagation are destined to become popular garden stalwarts. Others will languish or even be lost again.

Smooth stones in graduated sizes help define the paths and islands of moss and rhododendron in the garden of Trudy and Ian Dixon.

Suppose you learn about a new or unusual plant at a lecture, read its label at a botanical garden, then overhear its name whispered in hushed respect at the Garden Club meeting; you want it. If the local garden center doesn't have it, and the seeds aren't in the big seed catalogs, where else can you turn? Specialty nurseries usually compile and sell catalogs with valuable plant descriptions, cultivation suggestions, and, of course, the opportunity to order the plants. To find these nurseries, read the small advertisements in local gardening magazines, and watch for them at the large garden shows. Botanical gardens often have plants for sale either in a shop or at huge spring sales, great for unusual plants and good bargains. Horticultural societies focus on specific plant groups, such as rhododendrons, bonsai, alpines, even palms. Watch for their yearly sales; many of the plants offered are unavailable anywhere else.

The lure of plants from the temperate mountainous regions of Asia and South America is not only their novelty but also the possibility that these plants will prove to be garden-worthy. Plants from places with high rainfall and the consequent acid soil are likely to do well here. In fact, given enough time, many plants would migrate round the world (via birds and winds) and populate distant lands without the help of plant hunters. This is an ongoing process, as plants that were wiped out by glaciation in the Ice Ages are still returning, albeit at a very slow pace. Often plants from far-flung regions—the hostas of Japan, the rhododendrons of China, the epimediums, kirengashomas, and lilies from temperate forests around the world—fit so well in a shaded naturalistic garden, they look as though they could be native species here.

Plants of the Pacific Northwest are still being discovered and introduced into the horticulture trade. Double-flowered forms of salmonberry (*Rubus parviflorus*), thimbleberry (*R. spectabilis* 'Olympic Double'), and a curly rush (*Juncus* 'Unicorn') found by botanist-hikers are available from specialty nurseries, and more will surely come.

Just as rhododendrons are the most beloved of flowering shrubs in the region, hostas must surely be the most sought-after perennial. Despite the allure of their broad leaves to slugs and snails, it seems that every shade gardener finds hostas beguiling. With leaf colors from blue-green through emerald and yellow, contrasting markings of white or golden edges or centers, flame-like patterns, surfaces that are puckered, ribbed, quilted, or smooth, leaf sizes from gerbil to raccoon, hostas in their boundless variations are collectible plant pets. The large ones especially can anchor a planting of more delicate foliage or less distinctively organized leaves. The golden or variegated species or cultivars may bring a welcome levity among darker foliage or in dull shade. Grouped, their diversity can be appreciated in a sort of shrine to green.

All garden plants are descended from wild species. Some that we grow are still in their original form, but many others are hybrids or cultivars bred or selected for desirable qualities such as flower size, markings or color, leaf variegation, overall plant shape or size, or even the speed or slowness of their growth. While the plant breeders offer us more and more choices of designer

Nine ways to tackle slugs

1. Snip 'em with scissors.
2. Stomp 'em underfoot.
3. Drop 'em in a pot of beer.
4. Fling 'em into the sea.
5. Search for them and their eggs under logs, rocks, and pots.
6. Check under their favorite plants often.
7. Collect egg shells to sprinkle around susceptible plants in spring.
8. Hunt for them on dewy mornings, rainy days, and in mild winter and spring weather.
9. Shrug and accept some slug damage. It's only natural.

The shapely, felted leaves and compact growth habit of *Rhododendron yakushimanum* and its hybrids are as important to their beauty as the flower trusses.

plants, some plant collectors prefer to grow the unimproved—or unadulterated—species, finding more to celebrate in the handiwork of nature than of humans.

Some of the finest rhododendron hybridizers are working in British Columbia, Washington, and Oregon, creating new cultivars with long-blooming, showy flower trusses and compact growth. But gardeners such as Glen Patterson delight in the originals, growing species conifers, alpines, and rhododendrons. He strives in his rocky West Vancouver garden to distill the essence of a mountain forest and an alpine scree. His rhododendrons range in size from inchling ground-huggers with minute foliage to fast-growing giants with leaves a foot (thirty centimetres) long. Rather than seeking the biggest and boldest flowers, Glen enjoys observing the infinite variations of scent, leaf color, texture, and shape, the adaptations of plants to their differing native homes, and the often more modest flower trusses, which he deems more suitable to a garden inspired by nature. For him as for other rhodophiles, the new plant explorations offer exciting opportunities.

At the seashore the spirit of place is in the ever-changing water and open sky, rocky outcroppings, gnarly shore pines and twisted arbutus trees, the salty wind and inevitable downward slope. For gardeners, the moist salt air is usually a blessing, moderating temperatures and providing extra humidity during summer drought, which is particularly acute on the San Juan and Gulf Islands. Some garden plants cannot survive the salt, so it makes good sense to retain the native trees, shrubs, and grasses found near the sea. Soil is usually thin, sandy, and very fast-draining in these areas. Seaside gardeners often amend their soil vigorously, using leaves, garden and kitchen waste, and seaweed to make as much compost as they can. Hummock-shaped Mediterranean plants such as sage, low grasses, pinks, heaths, and heathers echo the simple rounded shapes of boulders and rocky knolls without obscuring the sea view. The statuesque silhouettes of such plants as spiky

Remarkable rhododendrons

With hundreds of rhododendrons available now, consider the year-round qualities of the shrubs. There are taller, open-growing ones and shorter, more compact ones, varying leaf sizes and colors, as well as many appealing flower forms and colors. All require good drainage and, during dry spells, watering at their roots. Don't be intimidated by the Latin names; most of the employees in the garden centers can't pronounce them either. The first ones listed are not difficult to find.

- *Rhododendron impeditum* is a very small shrub with tiny gray-green scaly leaves and masses of variably mauve to purple flowers in April or May. It can withstand full sun, keeps its petite size, and is ideal for a rockery or small garden. In winter its leaves seem brighter against the dark wet soil.
- *R. yakushimanum* has leathery, convexly curved leaves with woolly white hairs beneath (called *indumentum*), dark pink buds that pale as they open to white bells, and a tidy, dense growth habit ideal in smaller gardens. After flowers fade, new shoots emerge covered with a silvery wool (called *tomentum*) like a second flush. All of the many yak hybrids (such as 'Yaku Princess') are good bets.
- *R. augustinii* and its hybrids (such as 'Blue Diamond' and 'Electra') are some of the best blue- to violet-flowered medium-sized rhodos, and are stunning massed.
- *R. decorum* grows to be a large shrub or small tree with white or pink-tinged bell-shaped flowers. The new shoots are glaucous, the mature bark fissured, and the flowers highly scented.
- *R. schlippenbachii* is a deciduous azalea-type rhododendron from Korea whose delicate, pale pink, funnel-shaped flowers bloom before the leaves emerge. Good autumn color.
- *R. falconeri* grows to fifty feet (fifteen metres) in its native Himalayan region, and has impressive foot-long (thirty-centimetre), dark shiny leaves with cinnamon indumentum underneath; a grand shrub for a large woodland garden. Like the similar *R. macabeanum* it needs a location protected from winter winds. Both bear huge, creamy yellow flower trusses.

New Zealand flax, shore pine, or arbutus gain strength as the light accentuates their more complex shapes.

One of the most sensitive ways to use plants is to select them for their resonance, that is, the ideas of nature that their shapes or textures bring to mind. Weeping plants evoke falling water, tall arching grasses are fountain-like, foamy plants may bring to mind the sound and motion of splashing water.

The lively forms of umbrella pine (*Sciadopitys verticillata*) and two grasses, *Miscanthus sinensis,* and, lower *Helictotrichon sempervirens* edge a bridge in Kathy Poole's garden.

A rushing stream cuts through the steep garden of Kathy Poole, roaring insistently as water bounces from rock to rock. As an artist, Kathy is interested in using plants in ways that exploit the form of each plant, regardless of its familiarity or rarity. More important is its overall shape and mass, that is, the volume it occupies and the density of its foliage. To respond to the water's character visually, Kathy uses several striking plants for their water-like qualities. Ornamental grasses mark the beginning of a route that follows the stream's downward course. On breezy days, the grasses wave, and even when the air is still, their fluid shapes impart a sense of motion. The path crosses the stream twice on wooden bridges, and culminates under huge tropical leaves of *Gunnera manicata.* The delicate radiating lines of the grasses and an umbrella pine echo the spraying, splashing qualities of the stream. Along the stream's edge, Kathy employs a mass of two very common plants, frothy lady's mantle and yellow Welsh poppy. At the foot of the garden is a playful upset of the notion of scale. From above, gunnera leaves look big, but as you approach and then pass beneath them, you are dwarfed by their immensity, like Alice in Wonderland. Using proportion, scale, form, and space, Kathy's garden plays with many of the facets of both water and plants.

In Japanese gardening, each plant, rock, pond, or stream represents some aspect of nature. By abstracting the qualities of natural scenes—the cragginess of a steep mountain pass, the tranquility of a calm lake, the tumult of a stormy seashore, the majesty of a still forest—the Japanese show their deep respect for nature.

I find it ironic that the world's most carefully contrived garden style is so closely associated with nature. To a greater extent than in North America, a garden in Japan, even a small home garden, is considered a form of art.

In a natural meadow, part of Robert and Birgit Bateman's Gulf Island garden, thin meadow soil supports a wealth of flora and fauna. River otters beat paths through the grass, and these the Batemans supplement with mown swaths.

forest and meadow

When wildlife artist Robert Bateman began making a garden on Salt Spring Island, his goal was not to tame the existing landscape, but to make a garden useful for his family, keeping much of the existing meadowland intact, while carefully manipulating it in places to evoke natural habitat. The rocky meadows rich in grasses and wildflowers are little disturbed by the narrow footpaths mown through them. With the help of landscaper Tom Hall, Robert made a bit of rain forest under the loose canopy of Garry oaks, arbutus, and Douglas firs.

They rerouted a small creek through a bed painstakingly formed using both existing boulders and concrete "rock" they molded themselves. This shady, cool oasis attracts a wealth of birds to the stream, its pools, and a generous bird feeder. Many of the smaller plants – native sword, deer, and licorice ferns – were transplanted from elsewhere on the property.

The success of the shade garden is due in part to the Japanese idea of a stroll garden. The circuitous pathway causes you to pause and view the parts of the garden from specific spots that take full advantage of the natural and created features.

gardening in scale

Jocelyn Horder's Puget Sound home and garden seem to nestle into the foreshore, hugging the land above high tide. The low, brick, pavilion-style buildings are unobtrusive, complementing the landscape. Between house and sea Jocelyn had once hoped to have a meadow garden, but the land proved too mucky and wet. Designer Dan Robinson made a series of rock and soil mounds that preserved the low-lying character but allowed slow-growing or creeping conifers and small shrubs and groundcovers, such as evergreen azaleas, lavender, sedum, and moss, to thrive between the boulders and driftwood. Gravel paths wander about the sculpted mounds, which are just high enough to obscure what grows on the far side, leading you on to discover what that hint of purple might be.

The small garden behind the house has the same sense of a naturalistic sculpture, but the scale is larger. Mature Japanese maples and open-pruned pines balance massive mossy boulders. Huge stumps appear to have fallen where they lie, with native huckleberries and salal growing densely about them. Vibrant green deer ferns, both our native *Blechnum spicant* and tiny-fronded *B. penna-marina* from South America and New Zealand, and shiny black mondo grass (*Ophiopogon planiscapus* 'Nigrescens') carpet the ground.

In an adjacent outdoor room behind a brick wall, Jocelyn tends her extensive bonsai collection. As she is no longer able to prune her large trees herself, she continues to practice her art in miniature, where each leaf and twig garners attention. Here the garden's scale is intimate, but the experience and pleasure of emulating nature just as fulfilling.

It involves more representation, more abstraction, more artifice. A Japanese Zen rock garden looks at first very unnatural to Western eyes, but it evokes nature intellectually and spiritually.

Our climate and terrain are quite similar to those of Japan so our coastal gardens can readily adapt many of the Japanese gardening principles. They are not blueprints, but fundamentals of the art of garden-making based on *in* and *yo,* the Japanese counterparts of Taoist *yin* and *yang.* The artistic distillation or simplification of nature's complexity is the design goal, but underlying this is a profound desire to understand our role in the universe. Asymmetrical balance, the use of complementary qualities such as light and dark, fine and coarse textures, hard and soft materials, and the manipulation of our perception of space all play a role, as do the many natural cycles of change and renewal. Japanese-style gardens have been a strong counter-influence to our European gardening heritage. In turning away from what some perceive as an over-reliance on flowery English cottage gardens and maintenance-intensive lawns, Western gardeners have looked to the Orient to find other models. But since the culture of North America is so different from that of Japan, to copy Japanese gardens too literally or without understanding may result in a design that refers only to Japan instead of to nature.

In Woodinville, Washington, Japanese-trained garden designer Terry Welch has created a garden influenced by Japanese precepts yet thoroughly rooted in his specific site, its flora, fauna, history, and mythology. The boundaries between cultivated and uncultivated land are blurred; garden merges with wilderness, and emerges from it. He has cleared some sections over a period of years, reshaping the land in places, planting wide shrubby borders around the margins of two large beaver ponds. (The whole garden is twenty acres/eight hectares, about one-fifth of it cultivated.) Against a backdrop of second-growth cedars, firs, hemlocks, and red alders, he has planted non-native trees—katsura and Himalayan birches, dawn redwoods and weeping California sequoias, broad-leafed evergreens and conifers—for delight through all four seasons. In the Japanese tradition, Terry utilizes the tension and balance of rocks and water, vertical shapes and horizontals, rectilinear

Above:
Terry Welch's Zen garden is open to the surrounding landscape. Its formality may stir intellectual or spiritual contemplation of nature.

Opposite:
Lavender and other low plants form hummocks in the garden of Jocelyn Horder.

By the bell at the entrance to Terry Welch's garden, forms and textures of evergreen groundcovers, shrubs, and trees set a calm, welcoming tone all year, even in late fall, when turning maples provide lively color contrast to the many greens. A dignified Japanese red pine (*Pinus densiflora*), lacy Japanese maples (*Acer palmatum* 'Ever Red' at left and *A. palmatum* 'Viridis Group', center), dense rhododendrons, and creeping between the huge stepping-stones, the ruffled leaves of *Rubus pentalobus* all contribute detail and variety to the scene.

architecture and curved lawns, spaces that open up and close again. An Indonesian structure at water's edge is a contemplative place to observe the resident frogs and dragonflies, the ducks and beaver. It also functions like a Japanese tea house. The path of granite stepping-stones floating in moss that leads to the pavilion refers to the walk of cleansing and spiritual receptivity that precedes the tea ceremony.

Near the center of the property on the crest of a low hill, a Zen garden follows the Japanese tradition of using large, deep-seated rocks as islands in a sea of waves raked in the gravel. However, to this usually closed form, a universe contained, Terry added the North American value of openness, leaving two sides of the Zen garden unwalled so it can be viewed from within or without, integrated with the larger landscape. In doing so he has welcomed the footprints of deer, coyote, and on one special day, the eggs of a turtle.

As Terry continues to shape this land, he is increasingly aware of being one of many creatures that occupy the land, and the importance of the garden as sanctuary. He finds resonance in the mythology of the Snoqualmie people who inhabited the region historically, connections between their stories and his own life. There are parallels, in the Zen garden and even within the details of an individual bonsai, between the garden and its grand setting of mountains and rivers beyond.

The structural elements used to shape a garden—the paths, steps, retaining walls, arbors, fences, patios, and furniture—are of course manufactured additions. In the naturalistic garden, well-chosen materials can make a positive contribution to the sense of partnership with nature. In a rocky garden where faces of stone cleared of brush and debris reveal their timeless character, there are likely a sufficient number of movable stones to use as steps, or to be piled without mortar to make soil pockets for planting. Holding a stream bed or making a Japanese stone bridge needs bigger, more sculptural rocks and the assistance of hired machinery. These large building blocks may be purchased, but require care and subtlety for their selection and placement.

Where the forest gives the garden its personality, heavy square timbers or upright log segments are fitting materials for arbors or small retaining walls.

Growing under cedars

Many despair at attempting to grow anything under large western red cedars, which are greedy for nutrients and moisture. Their widespread fine roots form a dense mat in the soil, making it difficult for other plants to compete, and the rust-colored scaly leaves that carpet the soil directly below the trees in fall inhibit germination and growth. Sunshine Coast gardener Stuart Webber recommends these ways to grow successfully under cedars.

- Remove the lowest branches to admit adequate light and air.
- Clear away as much of the cedar droppings as possible. They make a good weed-suppressing mulch for pathways.
- To plant, dig a hole wider than usual, using a sharp spade to cut through the cedar roots. Add fresh soil. Water well to establish new plants, as little rainfall will penetrate the cedar's crown.
- Top-dress with additional soil, well-rotted compost and/or manure each winter.
- Control the spread of cedar roots by digging out spades full of matted soil between established plants each winter, replacing with new soil. Think of it as akin to aerating a thatched lawn.
- Choose shade- and acid-tolerant plants: shrubs such as rhododendron, kalmia, or mahonia; large perennials such as ferns, astilbe, hosta, or Solomon's seal; groundcovers such as hardy geraniums, omphalodes, or periwinkle, and tiny treasures such as cyclamen, colchicum, or violets.

Unpainted split or sawn cedar boards make woodsy gates and fences; saplings or cedar branches stripped of their bark are rustic handrails. If wooden boards or log rounds are used for walkways or steps, the surface may be made slip-proof by affixing half-inch (one-centimetre) wire grid or even chicken wire with heavy-duty staples.

Sun-bleached driftwood adds character to coastal or island gardens, as do benches and structures made from timbers that float ashore. In Japanese-style gardens, the flexible strength of bamboo balances rigid wood and stone.

Other materials, available from a building supply center, are useful for their invisibility. Reinforcing bar (usually called rebar or rerod), for instance, is very versatile for pegging wooden steps in place, supporting a trellis, or staking plants. Outdoors, the metal quickly rusts, so it recedes visually and is less noticeable than wooden supports. On steep slopes, six-inch (fifteen-centimetre) wire grid may be laid and secured with rebar to retain the soil while groundcovers take hold. Flexible black plastic pipe can be used as an invisible arch (with rebar inserted in the uprights) for vines, and even chain-link fencing with a dark matte finish may make an unseen barrier to keep dogs and other animals in (or out). Unlike shiny materials that are spotlighted when the sun or even the sky is reflected on their surface, these dark neutral materials never obtrude.

Paths, too, may be formed with materials chosen to complement their surroundings while meeting the needs of foot traffic. Materials that relate to the garden as a whole are most easily integrated. There is no more beautiful material than moss for woodland paths with light traffic; for sturdier wear, use bark mulch or fallen needles, even the autumn litter from western red cedar trees. Stone paths suit rocky gardens and give a garden a look of venerability; gravel fits into either wet or dry meadows, and has the added benefit of allowing seeds to germinate easily for transplanting. Many gardeners now use black landscape cloth under their mulch paths to suppress weeds, but unless this is very carefully laid, the cloth will soon emerge in places where rocks or tree roots are near the surface and the mulch is thin.

Paul and Margaret Daniels encouraged native moss to establish on shady steps and paths.

woodland hillside

To plant the slopes of her woodland garden, Margaret Daniels needed innovative techniques. On gentle inclines she put in cuttings of such quick-rooting groundcovers as dead nettle and ajuga. These fast-spreading plants hold the surface soil yet are easily pulled when they extend beyond their allotted space, while the deep roots of large trees hold the subsoil in place.

Where the slope is formidably steep, she and her husband, Paul, placed six-inch (fifteen-centimetre) wire grid secured with rebar, both leftovers from house construction, to stabilize the new groundcovers and provide footing during the initial planting and later gardening. It was a daunting task. Pre-loosened plant pots were tossed from above, caught, and planted with one hand while the other clung to the grid. Although Margaret worried that the wire mesh would show forever, it was covered with leaves in a few months.

Using patches of moss already there, Paul established colonies of moss wherever possible, transplanting hunks of it along shady walkways, in chinks in walls, on earthen steps. Purchased mosses were less successful, but the extant varieties soon made living carpets that inspire barefoot walks. The maintenance moss requires is not unreasonable – clearing debris frequently in autumn and picking out weed seedlings from time to time. Summer drought distresses but does not kill the moss, and it revives with a light sprinkling from hose or rain shower.

If the goal is a path that looks natural, it may be better to omit the cloth but resolve to weed the gravel or mulch from time to time. In rare situations, crushed blue-black mussel or white oyster shells are available in sufficient quantity to make a short seaside path. Exposed aggregate, concrete, or paving tiles may be the most suitable materials in city gardens or wherever an even footing is needed. Mown grass, too, makes a surprisingly natural living path in a garden with sufficient sunlight to support it.

Water is the element that universally befits the naturalistic garden. The most powerful and insistent force of nature here is the Pacific Ocean and the moisture carried on its winds, falling as rain as the air ascends the mountains. In our gardens, water may rush in existing or created streams that echo those that tumble down mountain slopes, or may lie in ponds still as ocean inlets on a foggy morning. Water in a garden unerringly recalls water in nature.

The surface of a pond is a simple horizontal plane, making a negative space, an absence or openness, a rest amid the complexity of plants, a serenity. Where branches overhang and many different plants crowd around, a strong sense of the pond as natural system exists. Where large rocks or smaller pebbles make a simpler pattern, its beauty is more formal, more intellectual. A pond holds fascination because its mood changes as the reflected light shifts from spring to fall, from sunshine to storm, from dawn to twilight.

A stream too has an individual character determined by its incline, the course it follows, the rocks that contain it, the rate of flow, its sound, shape,

Water ways

Ponds may be made with sealed concrete or prefabricated plastic liners. They look most uncontrived at a low point in the garden, where water might pool naturally. If a pond is not practicable, consider using an urn or glazed ceramic pot to enjoy the benefits of reflection and light.

In-pond plants usually stay in their black plastic pots resting on blocks to raise them to the desired height. Marginal plants, that is, the ones that grow at the edges, need moist roots all year, especially in the growing season, but most plants cannot stand waterlogged conditions. Soil for these plants needs to be moisture retentive, but moderately well drained. More drought-tolerant plants can also be used, slightly uphill from the marginals.

The natural stream that rushes down Kathy Poole's hillside animates the garden with its constant roar and vigorous tumble.

splash, even the smell of the air around it. Those lucky enough to have a naturally occurring stream may observe extreme seasonal fluctuations, from thundering, perhaps threatening winter cascade to benign summer trickle. Where the stream depends on a hidden pump system, the flow may be more manageable, but equally gratifying. Like a pond, or in combination with one, a stream draws the viewer into its life, inviting observation, memory, association, contemplation, metaphor, spirituality.

These are the deeper rewards of naturalistic gardening at its best, but even in its simpler forms, growing plants that remind us of forest or meadow and shaping the land in ways that imitate rather than conquer nature, we can know the pleasure of taking our cues from the land itself.

Focus on Foliage

A reassuring mid-green dominates our landscape all year—the glossy emerald of laurel and the dull leather of arbutus, the sometimes warm, often somber green boughs of western red cedar, and except in the dry regions created by mountain rain shadows, the ubiquitous green of mossy lawns. Most winters this verdure is erased by only a few days of snow, after which the greenery seems positively to glow. Since almost every garden scheme depends on its range of foliage plants, we should consider how they work with buildings, garden structures, and the surrounding scenery as well as with each other. And because we venture into our gardens in any month, not just the flowery ones, we depend on *all* the qualities of our plants—the blooms of course, but also leaves, berries, seed heads and other fruits, the overall form and mass of the plants, the color and texture of bark, and when winter drops her deciduous cloak, the elegant tracery of branches sparkling with raindrops against leaden skies. Clever gardeners compose with all these qualities in mind.

Our relatively benign maritime climate presents us with a range of planting possibilities that can be at once inspiring and bewildering. Our nurseries, once dominated by hanging basket standbys such as petunias and trailing lobelia, now display scores of perennials, ornamental grasses, tempting herbs, shrubs, groundcovers, many newly available species, and novel varieties of old favorites. Even experts must frequently check their reference books and journals.

OPPOSITE:
In her Kirkland, Washington, border, gifted gardener Eleanor Carnwath shows that beautiful and varied foliage is the backbone of a lovely planting. The white flowers of *Hydrangea macrophylla* 'Lanarth White' appear more chaste near the broad blue leaves of *Hosta* 'Buckshaw Blue' and the bright blue berries and red stems of *Diphylleia cymosa*. Varied leaf shapes and plant heights enliven the composition.

ABOVE:
Perennial hellebore (*Helleborus foetidus*) and umbrella pine tree (*Sciadopitys verticillata*) have a similar pattern of foliage in Kathy Leishman's garden.

A sunny terrace and broad steps give a Mediterranean character to Susan Ryley's Victoria, B.C., garden. Gray-leafed plants abound – *Teucrium fruticans* 'Azureum', *Santolina chamaecyparissus* (cotton lavender), and in the blue-green pot, *Salvia chamaedryoides*. The silvers contrast with green and gold ivy (*Hedera helix* 'Buttercup'), which provides balance.

As in most aspects of our culture, we are fast developing a regional style that refers to strong influences from other places. The English traditions of abundant, informal cottage plantings and sweeping, park-like landscape gardens are suitable here, as are carefully crafted Japanese-style gardens made mostly of rocks and shrubs. Especially in sunny, south-facing gardens, we find Mediterranean and Californian influences of silver-leafed plants and oversized pots overflowing onto paved terraces. More recently gardeners have experimented with desert succulents, tropical palms, and meadow grasses, always tempered by our regional context of dependable year-round greenery. But the most innovative gardeners begin by examining the existing landscape, its native plants and intrinsic character, and draw the most appropriate elements, including plants, from any tradition they wish.

There are two very different styles that take full advantage of the effects of foliage. One favored by landscape architects is the massed plantings that make a definitive statement with a very limited number of plant types. Blocks of a dozen or more hostas or sword ferns, for instance, have great impact. Many home gardeners, however, want to grow a wider variety of plants, so choose instead a more complex tapestry style. Either a small clump or just one of each plant is sited with reference to its many varied neighbors. Plant addicts and collectors are more likely to choose the latter, more detailed style, whereas more architecturally oriented gardeners may prefer using plants as larger sculptural blocks. Even in the most eclectic of gardens, repeated use of one plant or color brings rhythm and unity.

Most evergreens—conifers, heather, bamboo, and broad-leafed shrubs such as rhododendron and holly—are year-round stalwarts that together with paths, fences, and other structures form the overall garden configuration, often called the *bones*. But throughout the seasons, the leaves of other plants contribute liveliness, form, depth, and intriguing detail to the garden picture.

Choosing a plant for its foliage qualities, then grouping plants in the garden to enhance each one's appearance, is a challenge. Garden designers often think first of terms such as "vertical-habit shrub" or "massed, low, drought-tolerant grasses" rather than listing the specific plants they'll use. Every plant should be selected also for its suitability to the growing conditions of the site—light, moisture, soil type, and hardiness—but many different plants might fit the bill.

Spikes and spears of long, thin (lanceolate) leaves may either arch gracefully, as do daylilies and most ornamental grasses, or rise in stiff lines radiating from the base, as with yuccas and most irises. Used singly, New Zealand flax (*Phormium tenax*) is a punctuation mark, even an exclamation. A six-foot (two-metre) clump of the grass *Miscanthus sinensis* is uplifting, lyrical. Groups of iris make a perky, upright effect, pleasing before and after their brief bloom time. To a billowy cloud of hardy geraniums, the iris leaves lend stability. Used near decks, patios, or steps, lanceolate leaves balance the horizontal lines.

Large leaves proclaim, Here I am! Beside plants with smaller leaves, they provide the eye with a place to rest, an anchor that prevents a garden from being busy or chaotic. *Gunnera* (affectionately but wrongly called giant

Opposite:
The shimmering blue bracts of *Cerinthe major* 'Purpurascens' provide as much interest as its flowers.

rhubarb) is the biggest, boldest perennial I know—so big, it is difficult to site in home gardens. Like many other plants with oversized, flat leaves, it needs a constant supply of moisture for optimum health. For a boggy garden, species of *Ligularia, Rodgersia, Darmera,* or native skunk cabbage make a strong statement. Large-leafed hostas are more tolerant of drier conditions and deserve their popularity, adding mass and dignity to a planting. Windmill palms (*Trachycarpus fortunei*) and banana trees have large, bold leaves and impart a tropical, even holiday mood, but both may need a burlap wrapping during our coldest weather.

Tiny leaves have an ethereal quality because the eye cannot fix on any one leaf. Masses of pinpoint leaves draw attention to overall plant texture, color, and shape, as in a Pointillist painting, and balance strong shapes such as tree trunks or boulders. *Lonicera nitida* 'Baggesen's Gold' and box (*Buxus sempervirens*) are good tiny-leafed shrubs and can be clipped into topiary shapes.

Good plants your mother didn't tell you about

- *Hakonechloa macra* 'Aureola' is a gracefully arching, low-growing golden grass from Japan. Partial shade.
- *Kirengeshoma palmata* is another Japanese perennial with elegant dark stems, light green leaves and waxy yellow bell flowers in August. *K. koreana* has larger, more open flowers. Partial shade.
- *Metasequoia glyptostroboides* (dawn redwood) is a very fast-growing – to a hundred feet, or thirty metres – fat-trunked deciduous conifer discovered in 1941, in a valley in China. Full sun in a large garden.
- *Athyrium niponicum* 'Pictum' (Japanese painted fern) animates a shade garden with its silver and green fronds on red stems. Shade. The selection of available ferns of varying sizes, colors, and textures is wonderful.
- *Helichrysum petiolare,* annual in this climate, has small, felted gray leaves, suddenly popular as a container companion. 'Limelight' has lime-green leaves. Both are easy to propagate from cuttings and last until hard frost. Sun to part shade.
- *Crocosmia* (often called montbretia) and *Kniphofia* (red-hot poker) aren't news, but these newer cultivars are. *Crocosmia* 'Lucifer' is bright red and up to five feet (150 centimetres) tall; C. 'Solfatare' has bronze leaves and apricot flowers. Sun to partial shade. *Kniphofia* 'Ice Queen' is a tall, late-blooming version with yellow-ivory pokers, anything but red hot. Sun to partial shade. In many familiar plant families, new

cultivars are outperforming old.

- *Lathyrus odoratus* is the original species from which our garden sweet peas have descended. It is a small-flowered bicolor – moody blue and purple – that is more fragrant than most other sweet peas. This very bushy old-style cottage plant hasn't been easily available for years, but is listed anew in seed catalogs as 'Matucana'. Sun.
- *Cerinthe major* 'Purpurascens' is an annual, with iridescent purple-blue bracts and sea-green fleshy leaves. A bonus: it self-seeds. Sun.
- *Actinidia kolomikta* is a deciduous climber whose foliage is green, pink, and white. It's a close cousin of edible kiwi fruit, a very vigorous vine requiring a male and female plant for fruit production. Sun.
- *Agapanthus* 'Bressingham Blue' has strong strap-like leaves and cobalt flowers. It's only just hardy here, so needs deep winter mulch. It loves cramped spaces, so can be grown in a pot and wintered over in a garage. Sun.
- *Sorbus hupehensis* 'Pink Pagoda', a mountain ash introduced by the University of British Columbia Botanical Garden, is a deciduous tree that eventually grows to thirty feet/nine metres. It has white flower clusters in spring, blue-green leaves, and in late summer, pink berries. In fall the leaves turn orange and red, and in winter the berries pale to white. Sun to partial shade. UBC has developed dozens of new plant varieties available through garden centers.

Fine-textured *Artemisia* 'Powis Castle' complements the mauve stars of *Aster novi-belgii* 'Professor Kippenburg'.

Sweet woodruff (*Galium odoratum*) makes an ideal groundcover under larger rhododendrons. Its small, bright, evergreen leaves leaven the darker rhododendron foliage, and in spring woodruff bears thousands of frothy white flowers. Other fine-leafed groundcovers include periwinkle (*Vinca minor*), suitable for dry shade, and woolly thyme (*Thymus pseudolanuginosus*), a delightfully aromatic plant for sunny crevices in paving.

Extremely finely cut, feathery leaves have a high degree of detail. Cut-leaf maples, *Corydalis,* and maidenhair fern (*Adiantum pedatum*) have delicate, lacy leaf contours. Bronze fennel (*Foeniculum vulgare* 'Purpureum') appears like a plume of smoke rising moodily. *Santolina* and many artemisias bear extremely narrow, gray leaves, and the ferny foliage of annual cosmos looks more fragile than it is.

Plants with low mounding shapes invite purple prose. A clump of sea thrift (*Armeria maritima*) is a pink-flowered cushion. Tufts of blue fescue (*Festuca glauca*) are miniature fountains. Where spring- and fall-blooming heaths and heathers (*Erica* and *Calluna* species) are grouped together, they undulate in a colorful sea. To wry alpinists, *Androsace pyrenaica* is a tight bun. *Carex comans* is not a grass, but a bristly pet hedgehog.

If tiny leaves are like points, plants with needle-like leaves etch fine lines. Long-needled pines are at once strong and delicate forms. *Helleborus foetidus* has narrow, glossy, dark green leaves, completely different in character from pinks (*Dianthus*), which have finely cut, blue-gray leaves; both enhance nearby plants with more solid foliage.

Velvety gray or silver leaves shimmer in sunlight and bring a Mediterranean lightness to the garden. Like a velvet cloth, these leaves have a nap of tiny hairs that invite touch, so are favorites with children. Most silver, gray, or gray-green leaves, such as woolly lamb's ears (*Stachys byzantina*), *Senecio* 'Sunshine', or *Verbascum olympicum,* are also drought tolerant. The hairs help preserve the leaves' moisture. When backlighted, the hairs glow. When rain-soaked, the gray may disappear and reveal the green surface underlying the hairs. Willow-leafed pear (*Pyrus salicifolia* 'Pendula'), butterfly bush (*Buddleia davidii*), and the statuesque perennial plume poppy (*Macleaya*

Huge leaves of *Rodgersia podophylla* are an assertive element beside *Primula japonica* in the garden of Geri Barnes.

microcarpa) bring the silvery palette higher in the landscape. Silver-leafed plants are often used as companions for plants with soft mauve, pink, or white flowers. But gray and silver are equally useful in foliage compositions combined with golden, blue-green, and white-variegated foliage.

Leaves, of course, come in many colors. There are hundreds of variations in foliage hue—silver, gray, or steely blue; cream, golden, or wheat; blue-green, sea-green, or chartreuse; burgundy, purple, or red; ochre, copper, or bronze. Leaves may also be striped, mottled, spotted, blotched, rimed with white or gold, variegated in every possible way. The difficulty isn't in finding these colored-foliage plants but using them to advantage. Choosing a limited palette is one way. For instance, select several plants with mahogany leaves and/or flowers, and group them with plants with a chartreuse bias. Yellow-leafed plants may burn if given too much direct sunlight, but in dappled or open shade, their color is richer. White and cream variegated plants are good counterpoints to dark green, large-leafed plants, but if many variegated plants are used together, the effect may be chaotic. Variegation at the edge of large leaves emphasizes the leaf shape, as with *Hosta fortunei* 'Aureo-marginata'. Cream-and-green-striped *Phormium* 'Cream Delight' combines a strong form with lively coloration. *Cornus alba* 'Elegantissima' has soft green leaves edged irregularly in white, and the effect is much softer.

Moving, waving, rustling leaves animate the garden. Any plant bearing leaves or flowers at the end of thin branches or stalks sways readily with the slightest breeze, catching and reflecting light in all directions. The eye is drawn involuntarily to moving plants. Tall grasses, bamboo, and small-leafed deciduous trees are graceful performers. Silvery blue eucalyptus species are even livelier, but require a site protected from the coldest winter winds.

Shiny, hard-surfaced leaves act as mirrors, reflecting sunshine or the brilliance of an overcast sky. Although holly, laurel, salal, and *Mahonia* have dark green foliage, they may be dazzling in very bright light. This quality can be a feature or a distraction in foliage composition, and is too easily overlooked.

Architectural plants have special fascination in their growth patterns. The geometry of plants such as yuccas, *Eryngium giganteum*, or *Cotoneaster horizontalis* invites inspection to see how they are put together. Other plants are architectural simply because they are so much larger than others around them, such as huge clumps of ornamental grasses or the tall slender evergreen *Juniperus scopulorum* 'Skyrocket'. These act as landmarks in the garden's contour. When well placed among small-leafed plants, even the often misused yucca can unify disparate plantings.

How to put the plants together? The wonderfully diverse qualities of foliage present a happy challenge. Composing with leaves is a little like painting: it is easy to buy a variety of paints, but the possibilities for using them may be daunting, especially since, unlike paints on canvas, plants grow and change.

Bold leaf forms on *Phormium tenax, Acanthus mollis,* and *Colocasia esculenta* lend a tropical flavor to the garden of Tom Hobbs and Brent Beattie.

exotica

Inspired by the extravagance of Hollywood, Tom Hobbs and Brent Beattie of Southlands Nursery experiment in their home garden with tropical foliage, sensuous grasses, succulent rosettes, spikes, and spears, foliage of every color and habit. The plants may come originally from many diverse regions – windmill palm from China, European *Euphorbia* species, American desert yuccas, bronze New Zealand *Phormium tenax* – but they are melded to form a complex and richly textured sculpture.

Never satisfied, they continue to try new plants and bolder foliage forms. The tubers of taro (*Colocasia esculenta*) are tender and must be lifted for winter, but the drama of their purple-veined, arrow-shaped leaves beside the upright phormium is worth the effort.

a green tapestry

Pam Frost uses the broadest possible palette of greenery in this border, grouping together plants with similar cultivation needs. (These plants all thrive in partly shaded, well-drained loam amended every other winter with mushroom manure.) Then she plays with leaf forms, textures, and colors, looking for repetition or contrast.

The huge, rippled, blue-green leaves of *Hosta sieboldiana* 'Elegans' anchor this scene. Echoing their cool color is the frothy small-leafed rue, *Ruta graveolens* 'Jackman's Blue', whose texture is in turn echoed by the foamy chartreuse flowers of *Alchemilla mollis.* Yellow is repeated in the spotted leaves of *Persicaria virginiana* 'Painter's Palette' (left), the variegated leaves of a weigela shrub (background) and, in a few more weeks, tiny golden rue flowers. The ruddy *Heuchera* 'Palace Purple' foliage amplifies the coppery markings on the *Persicaria* leaves.

Recognizing your own responses to the shapes and textures is a good beginning. Certain plants call out to us from their pots in the garden center, yet others, perfectly healthy and perhaps very popular, do not. I cannot pass by donkeytail spurge (*Euphorbia myrsinites*) without admiring its twisting octopus arms of pointed, blue-gray leaves. A less architectural euphorbia, *E. dulcis* 'Chameleon', has rich, red-purple foliage, enjoys the same well-drained growing conditions, and provides a contrast in color and form. Together, both are better. At first, it is easier to use a few kinds of plants massed than to attempt a very complex picture. By trial and error, planting and digging up, revising the combinations and seeking more suitable companions, we very gradually build up a picture.

Seasoned Vancouver gardener Pam Frost has a method for integrating a plant into one of her borders. Some sections have moisture-retentive soil, some, more freely draining soil. In each, there are spots that receive more or less sunshine. When she acquires a new plant, she finds out as much as she can about its preferred growing conditions, then walks around the garden holding the pot against potential neighbors. Will its shape enhance the composition? Will the color of its leaves, petals, stamens, stems, or seeds echo a color found in adjacent plants? There are no hard rules, rather an intuition of what will likely work based on years of looking at plants. The new addition may have some surprises to offer, and its first location may well not be its permanent home.

Many plants have seasonal changes which add another dimension to the process of placing plants to best advantage. The dramatic foliage plants of summer may disappear in November, allowing their more modest evergreen neighbors an opportunity to show their worth. It is a rare gardener who has enough space to devote one section to the plants of spring, or another just to annuals. Most of us need to put plants together so there is a continuously pleasing overall picture, with some plants beginning their season of interest while others fade.

On a rare winter morning when snow has freshly fallen, the garden bones (or lack of them) are extremely obvious. This is an excellent day to make

OPPOSITE:
Plants in Pam Frost's border work as threads in a tapestry.

In autumn, the pleasingly arranged leaves of Solomon's seal (*Polygonatum biflorum*) glow golden in VanDusen Botanical Garden, Vancouver.

sketches or take photographs in the garden or from the windows of the house. But our winter cold spells are usually isolated islands in the continuum from late autumn to early spring. It isn't exceptional for the last roses to try to open their waterlogged buds while the first spring bulbs shoot up through the soil. Especially valuable foliage plants in winter include variegated holly (such as *Ilex aquifolium* 'Argentea Marginata'), hellebores (*Helleborus foetidus* and *H. argutifolius*), yellow conifers such as *Chamaecyparis pisifera* 'Filifera Aurea' or white-tipped *Cryptomeria japonica* 'Sekka-sugi', and kuma bamboo (*Sasa veitchii*).

In my garden, three small variegated plants provide the most pleasure—striped Japanese sedge (*Carex morrowii* 'Variegata'), white-edged ivy (*Hedera helix* 'Eva'), and *Arum italicum* 'Pictum', which has the refreshing habit of opening its lovely arrow-shaped leaves in autumn and keeping them all winter. After each winter rain the variegated kuma bamboo shimmers beneath the somber pines, cedars, and firs. Red-twig dogwoods (*Cornus alba* 'Spaethii') and red berries of holly and cotoneaster have impact in winter, when there are no flamboyant flowers to compete. And the conifers, majestic evergreen giants and elegant dwarf varieties, hold stately court through the winter.

I count the first warm day of the year, often in January, the start of spring. Although we may have snow as late as April, and there will undoubtedly be another two or three bouts of bitter Arctic winds, the signs of spring are undeniable. The exquisitely slow emergence and reawakening of plants is almost erotic. Each week brings new titillation—gray-green spikes of snowdrops, thick red snouts of peonies thrusting from the earth, prim purple curls of phlox shoots. Early foliage of columbines holds rainwater like crystals on dusty mauve-green doilies, and my special friends, the ferns, gradually release their tight-fisted spirals. Pulmonaria species bloom very early and may have solid green, white dotted, or silvery leaves. Last year's epimedium foliage is ready for a spring trim so that its delicate flowers may be more easily visible. As its new leaves appear, they may be marbled or tinged in red. Soon the garden's kaleidoscope has exploded to include every shade of green and a rainbow of spring bulbs. Late tulips may flower with early opening hosta leaves, but the leaves of some species tulips (such as

Playing with perspective

Choosing plants with graduated leaf sizes may make a garden appear larger by fooling the eye. A large-leafed shrub or small tree in the foreground with a small-leafed tree farther away will "stretch" perspective, making the small leaves seem very distant. For example, set the bold palmate leaves of evergreen *Fatsia japonica* at the garden entrance and, at the farthest visible point, a Japanese maple (*Acer palmatum*), with a plant in between bearing intermediate-sized leaves such as the perennial *Kirengeshoma palmata*. The size difference of the similarly shaped leaves will exaggerate the depth of the garden.

Tulipa kaufmanniana or *T. greigii*) may rival the hosta foliage with red stripes or wavy cream margins that make them welcome all season. Spears of iris rise fresh and optimistic.

Purple smoke bush (*Cotinus coggygria*) contrasts with Bowles' golden grass (*Milium effusum* 'Aureum') in VanDusen Botanical Garden.

By June, the garden picture may be dominated by flowers. But whether or not there are floral superstars present, every garden vignette depends on its cast of foliage plants to create harmony, add drama, and build the overall scene. Even more than flowers, foliage comes to life with the play of shifting light and shadow or the motion of the breeze. Gray-leafed plants such as Spanish lavender (*Lavandula stoechas*) or *Verbascum* species are at their best in dry summer weather, and glow buoyantly early and late in the day when the sun catches their leaves. The glaucous or blue-green leaves of *Euphorbia characias*, sea kale (*Crambe maritima*), and *Hosta sieboldiana* add a cooling note. Gold-leafed plants—golden full-moon maple (*Acer shirasawanum* 'Aureum'), Bowles' golden grass (*Milium effusum* 'Aureum'), or *Hosta* 'Sum and Substance', for example—bring levity to shadowy areas. Light-colored plants may also alter perspective by visually advancing, making adjacent darker plants seem farther away.

In midsummer, the sun high in the sky makes the garden flat and washed out at noon, but in early morning and late afternoon, light plays through the foliage of trees and shrubs in surprising ways. Before the sunlight reaches the garden, a cool blue cast falls over every plant. The sun's rays may illuminate a cobweb, spotlight an individual plant, or streak obliquely to intensify the contrast between sunny and shaded areas. As the sun sets, its low angle turns the garden briefly to gold. In the deepening blue of evening, most plants lose their distinctness, while pale flowers and silver leaves linger, glowing until moonset.

In autumn, as showier flowers begin to fade and more moisture is available through rain, fog, and dew, foliage seems refreshed and again draws our attention. The velvety silver leaves of *Artemisia ludoviciana* 'Valerie Finnis' glisten with dew against a darkening background. Yellow-leafed plants such as golden feverfew (*Tanacetum parthenium* 'Aureum') also take on new luster. Sugar maples that turn scarlet are not as common here as in eastern North

Witch alder (*Fothergilla gardenii*) shows its brilliant coloration in fall.

America, but many Japanese maples, Boston ivy (*Parthenocissus tricuspidata*), and *Euonymus alatus* provide brilliant reds. Fall colors vary widely from year to year and garden to garden. Last year's orange may this year be apricot or brown. A tree in full autumn glory on Halloween one year may turn at Thanksgiving the next. Even the order that plants color within a single garden varies. Deciduous rhododendrons, *Enkianthus,* and *Fothergilla* may be red-orange through orange and yellow. Leaves in every shade of gold can be found—hostas and Solomon's seal slowly turn to butter, grasses pale until they are wheat-colored, flowering cherries and big-leafed maple fade to gold. A very few—stag's horn sumac and *Parrotia persica,* for example—turn every shade from yellow through orange and red to deep purple.

But even while the spectacle of autumn color passes, the cedars and sword ferns, lawns and hedges keep the landscape a comfortable green. November is a month for admiring the deciduous trees. Stripped of their leaves, the branching patterns are revealed weeping or upright, complex or forthright.

great partnerships

Plants that originate from the same types of growing environments are always suitable mates. Choosing plants that will thrive in the conditions your garden offers is the best way to have healthy, vigorous plants that look their best. But bringing together plants that really sing is an art learned by observation and experimentation.

To practice matchmaking, pull a few leaves from two or three varied plants, and walk them around the garden. Hold the cut foliage against potential partners, watching for complements and contrasts. Some plants – Bowles' golden grass, golden feverfew, and bulbous oat grass, for instance – seem to enhance almost any planting. Others, such as *Persicaria virginiana* 'Painter's Palette', whose green leaves are randomly variegated in cream with red blotches, need sensitive associations.

Magnolias, rhododendrons, and other spring-flowering trees and shrubs have already fattened next year's flower buds.

Now we can see the spaces between trees more clearly, and the spaces within trees between branches as well. Before any pruning, it is wise to focus on these negative spaces. Pruning guides the direction of new growth, reshaping these spaces. To better understand the positive effects of negative-space pruning on both deciduous and evergreen trees and shrubs, visit a Japanese garden.

When I began to garden, I bought some seeds and flowers—poppies, snapdragons, nasturtiums. I didn't think of making a garden, only of having pretty, colorful blooms all summer. Then I saw some extraordinary gardens, notably those of Pam Frost of Vancouver and Elizabeth England of Victoria. I was astounded. The possibilities for using plants more fully began to open up. I started to see bloom as only one aspect of a plant, one plant as part of a vignette, and plant groupings as elements in a much larger, more exciting design. Elizabeth called it Leaf Gardening. Leaf gardeners do not forgo the beauty of bloom; in fact, they use the forms, colors, and scents of flowers in sometimes subtle, sometimes spectacular ways. But they do not use flowers in isolation, divorced from the plants that bear them or those which surround them. Neighboring plants may call attention to delicate markings, or echo the colors found on petals, sepals, pistils, and stamens.

As a photographer, this kind of gardening made sense to me. It is a great pleasure to observe, with or without a camera lens, the wonders of plants up close. As I moved the camera farther away from the flowers and leaves, I found delight in the relationships in plant communities and saw the plants in association with rocks, water, fences, paths, and buildings. It is an exciting journey, increasingly complex, yet always based on our evergreen landscape.

OPPOSITE:
Bulbous oat grass (*Arrhenatherum elatius* subspecies *bulbosum* 'Variegatum'), coral bells (*Heuchera* 'Pewter Moon'), and a spotted *Pulmonaria* seedling make a pleasing trio in Kathy Leishman's garden.

A Feast of Flowers

Sex in the garden, that's what flowers are all about. The plants that produce the flowers want only to procreate, and the infinite variations they find on this basic theme are admirable. The copious ways we find to take advantage of their beauty are equally admirable.

We use flowers to express joy at a wedding and solace at a funeral; to seduce, court, and earn forgiveness; to cement friendships, wow neighbors, and gain the respect of the Garden Club; to cheer the sick and reward the helpful; to demonstrate our horticultural prowess, our delight in bold color, our tasteful restraint; to recall childhood's wonder, evoke walks in alpine meadows, and keep close those who have moved or passed away; to please our senses, calm our anxieties, fuel an artistic spirit; to share with children, the aged, the not-yet-gardeners, strangers. Is there any end to the good reasons and right ways to grow flowers? Is it any wonder so many are lured into this voluntary slavery, and so few escape?

What a great treat it is to visit the private gardens of those brave souls who open their gates to garden tours. These are perfect opportunities to see what people have chosen to grow, which clematis looks superb twining through which magnolia, what, besides impatiens, blooms well in shade, how a tall delphinium is staked without obvious hardware, and how many different ways there are to use hardy geraniums. Every garden has its own quirks and style, and although the ones I visit may be vastly different from my own, and I may not want to imitate exactly what I see, I can always learn something valuable.

OPPOSITE:
Olga Towert's steep hillside is a stunning garden in a gully. Using many fast-spreading groundcover plants to hold the earth on the slope, Olga created fluid patterns and textures. Blue-flowered *Ajuga reptans,* pink native bleeding heart (*Dicentra formosa*), and white rock cress (*Arabis caucasica*) have been joined by clouds of self-seeded forget-me-nots (*Myosotis sylvatica*) to create a feast of flowers.

ABOVE:
A crocus flaunts its orange pistil.

In this sunny section of her small suburban garden, designer Clare Philips, owner of Phoenix Perennials in Vancouver, uses a cool palette: mauve *Nepeta* × *faassenii* 'Six Hills Giant' and *Scabiosa* 'Butterfly Blue', magenta *Geranium sanguineum,* blue *Delphinium cashmerianum,* and *Campanula persicifolia.* The yellow flowers of gray-leafed *Senecio* 'Sunshine' enliven the scene.

Mixed borders that use perennials, annuals, and grasses in combination with shrubs and even small trees are regarded by some as the pinnacle of flower gardening. (A border is defined as a long planting against something, often a hedge or fence. A double border is one that runs along either side of a central path.) Borders are highly complex, and if they make an effective show it is usually due to a great deal of planning, experimenting, and maintenance. Although each border is different, there are common themes. The broad-leafed evergreen and coniferous shrubs form a year-round backdrop of foliage and structure, so their placement is critical. Herbaceous plants, that is, ones without woody stems and which often die back to ground level in winter, are selected and placed based on their height, flower color, the qualities of their leaves, and through these, their complementary relationships to neighboring plants. Because color commands attention so readily, it is useful when studying a border to photograph it in black and white so that the interplay of forms is more apparent.

In the Vancouver Island country garden of Phoebe Noble, there are beds and borders of many shapes. (A bed differs from a border in that it is freestanding, not bordering anything.) Several borders are devoted to the many species and varieties of the plant she is best known for, the hardy geranium. In some areas of the garden she trials newly acquired geraniums to see how they will perform in sun or shade, how easily they spread or multiply, whether they stand up, grow in a mound, or flop about, how tall or compact they are, how they respond to her legendary midsummer mowing to encourage fresh new leaves and possibly a second flush of bloom, and so on. Another of the beds helps visitors identify geraniums, and there each one sports a label. But perhaps the most exquisite plantings are where the geraniums work as just one thread in a marvelous tapestry of flowering shrubs, vines, and perennials of many colors and shapes. By repeating certain plants throughout the garden—hardy geranium, allium, viburnum, maidenhair fern—Phoebe weaves infinitely varied threads into a unified fabric.

Unity may be established by the repeated use of one kind of plant, perhaps ferns, viburnums, or Japanese maples. Silver-, yellow-, or red-leafed

plants placed at regular or irregular intervals seem to converse with each other over distance, pulling together the disparate plants in between. Variety comes from differing plant shapes—spiky, mounded, columnar, or creeping, for example. Although most borders use a general arrangement of taller plants at the rear and shorter ones at the front, breaking this rigid order with tall plants at the front prevents it from being as boring as a class photo. A spike of woolly gray and yellow giant mullein (*Verbascum bombyciferum*) or a tall but open lilac veil of *Verbena bonariensis* or *Thalictrum delavayi* 'Hewitt's Double' adds height and interest without blocking the view of what lies behind.

At her summer cottage garden, Claire Wright wanted an abundant flower display without waiting years. She chose plants that grow quickly, including woolly lamb's ears (*Stachys byzantina*), lady's mantle (*Alchemilla mollis*), phlox (*Phlox paniculata*), and golden feverfew (*Tanacetum parthenium* 'Aureum'). Her signature hardy geraniums, blue-flowered *Geranium pratense* and pink-flowered *G. endressii*, spread with enthusiasm.

Opposite:
The author's seaside border is a playground for experimenting.

Color themes are as popular as ever—the silver and white border, the blue and yellow border, the border featuring apricot, copper, and terra cotta tones. In every case, the color and other qualities of foliage either detract from or support the chosen palette. The blue and yellow border, for instance, relies as much on plants with blue-green and yellow-green leaves as on plants with blue and yellow blooms.

One of the most common mistakes (one I made repeatedly) of new border-makers is to give the border insufficient depth. At my seaside garden, I first made a six-inch (fifteen-centimetre) strip of garden that ran along the width of the house in front of a deck. The border was backed by upright cedar boards, which had far more impact than any of the plants. Year by year I widened the strip in increasing increments, until one February I doubled it to seven feet (two metres). What a difference! Although it is still a small border, about twenty feet (six metres) long, it has room for several large plants, *Euphorbia characias, Phygelius* × *rectus* 'Moonraker', *Artemisia* 'Powis Castle', and *Rosa* 'Bonica', as well as dozens of smaller ones—bulbs, perennials, annuals, grasses, vines, an espaliered apple tree, a few herbs and vegetables, and some succulent groundcovers. Bees, butterflies, and birds are frequent visitors, especially hummingbirds, drawn to the nectar of columbines, *Phygelius,* bee balm, and delphinium. It's very full, and will need to be edited each year, removing plants that are no longer favorites, reducing the size of good but too-big plants by dividing them and giving away some of the divisions, or just making space for something new I wish to try. This is the challenge and the fun of it, for no border is static.

To plant, weed, trim, or deadhead the plants, you need a way of getting into the border without snapping off stems or compacting the soil over roots. A thick mulch acts as a cushion and lessens the impact of heavy footsteps. It also helps reduce evaporation from the soil and suppresses weed seedlings. Large borders usually have an access path running along the back or even through the middle. Unlike a main garden path, these are very narrow, rarely paved, and preferably invisible from the front of the border. Another solution is to use strategically placed stepping-stones, log rounds, or concrete blocks.

border building

I began this border years ago with a thin strip of oriental poppies right up against the boards. They were rewarding in their way – flamboyant hot orange flowers in late May – but hardly good year-round, or even all-summer plants, as their foliage quickly becomes messy and brown.

Each spring has seen satisfying advances of three types: an increase in the total area of the strip of earth, soil improvement through rigorous composting, and an expanding range of plants that integrates old favorites, including cosmos and woolly lamb's ears (*Stachys byzantina*), with new passions, such as long-blooming cape fuchsia (*Phygelius* × *rectus* 'Moonraker') and purple wallflower (*Erysimum* 'Bowles' Mauve'). Blue-green and yellow-green foliage plants such as *Euphorbia characias* and golden sage (*Salvia officinalis* 'Aurea') now play a bigger role, as do grasses and clematis, but I would not count this border a success unless it offered plenty of flowers for cutting and the enjoyment of visitors.

Bellevue Botanical Garden

The Bellevue Botanical Garden is a rising star in a region of great gardens; a visit is stimulating and instructive. Where hot-colored flowers set the border ablaze, big clumps of bronze-red daylilies with amber throats, red-hot pokers (*Kniphofia*) and scarlet *Crocosmia* 'Lucifer' are kindled by maroon-leafed barberry shrubs (*Berberis*). A few yards along, the heat is turned down a little, and a yellow segment depends heavily on the golden foliage of arching golden sedge (*Carex elata* 'Aurea') and golden creeping jenny (*Lysimachia nummularia* 'Aurea'). At first glance, the flowers often draw the most attention, but with only a little more observation, the many beautiful shapes, colors, and textures of the plants not in flower show their great strength and value to the border.

True xeriscaping, or dry gardening, is difficult in the Pacific Northwest because of our wet winter and spring. But with our dry summer weather, water-wise gardening is superb for any area, whether or not watering restrictions apply. One section of the Bellevue Botanical Garden is devoted to plants that require little watering. Here are some useful flowering plants for the water-wise garden.

- *Alchemilla mollis* (lady's mantle)
- *Buddleia davidii* (butterfly bush)
- *Coreopsis verticillata* (thread-leaf tickseed)
- *Cotinus coggygria* (smoke bush)
- *Geranium sanguineum* (bloody cranesbill)
- *Knautia macedonica* (crimson scabious)
- *Kniphofia uvaria* (red-hot poker)
- *Nepeta* × *faassenii* (catmint)
- *Salvia officinalis* (common sage)
- *Sedum* species
- *Stipa tenuissima* (Mexican feather grass)
- *Verbena bonariensis* (Brazilian verbena)

When I doubled the width of my border, I used pea gravel and flat rocks from the beach to form two equilateral triangles in the border, each side about three feet (one metre), with the pointed end just even with the front. As the season advances, the triangles disappear visually, but still enable me to reach most plants without stepping on the soil. A ceramic pot of blue oat grass sits on each gravel triangle, contributing variation in texture; in winter and spring, their shapes add much-needed structure.

One of the largest, most spectacular borders in the world, the impressive undertaking of a cadre of volunteers, is at the Bellevue Botanical Garden in Bellevue, Washington. The border is huge, 22,000 square feet (2000 square metres), and has room for many moods and themes. A path of hazelnut shells leads into the middle, so visitors can immerse themselves.

In small gardens, the scale is quite different. Each plant, each bloom, gains importance. There are fewer of them, and each one is viewed more closely. The overall sweeping pattern may be lost, but the impact of a well-orchestrated grouping may be great.

One way city-lot gardeners scale down the big border is to make clusters of well-chosen plants in small beds. An advantage of this is that fewer plants combine more easily to good effect. In a five-foot square (1.5 by 1.5 metre) bed there is room for a tall grass or slender shrub, three or four medium-sized perennials that bloom at different times, some tight low plants, and something looser to flop forward. A trellis could support a vine or two. In the soil between these plants there might also be bulbs that come up, bloom, and fade without interfering with the other plants. Such a planting requires much less time to maintain, but every few years, some plants may need to be dug up and divided so they don't war with each other. With so many plants in a small space, feeding them is critical, and an annual top-dressing of compost or manure may not be enough. As with containers, organic liquid food is very useful, applied in weak solution.

Plants with lax stems cannot support their own weight, but they grow in a variety of charming ways that bring motion and liveliness into the garden. Low creepers have stems with roots at intervals, and are just right for filling

ABOVE:
The borders at the Bellevue Botanical Garden are a major project of the Northwest Perennial Alliance. Designers Carrie Becker, Bob Lilly, Charles Price, and Glenn Withey combined some of the finest plants available in fluid drifts of colors, leaf forms, and growth habits that explore the full range of planting possibilities.

OPPOSITE:
Drought-tolerant plants at the Bellevue Botanical Garden stay healthy and attractive without supplementary watering.

Above:
Lysimachia nummularia 'Aurea' illuminates darker foliage along a gravel path at Heronswood Nursery, Kingston, Washington.

Opposite:
Raised boxes surround Audrey Litherland's wooden deck.

in the spaces between pavers or carpeting the ground between shrubs. Plants that flop will lean gracefully over the edge of a wall, reaching forward, or dangle delicate flowers like hanging bells. Vines need an appropriate support to grow upward through a tree, on a trellis or arbor, on a chain hanging from an eaves or along the fascia board of the house. Most clematis, for example, have twining tendrils to attach themselves to their support, but climbing roses need the assistance of ties to hold their heavy flowering canes.

Another style that works well in patio or rooftop gardens is putting all the plants in large containers. A fine example of this is the garden of Audrey Litherland. As the house builder had buried the really good soil under yards of fill, Audrey had a series of large oblong boxes constructed to hold much of her garden. Placed at the perimeter of a wide wooden deck, they act like a privacy hedge, raising plants high enough to hide passersby from view. She refused to be limited in her choice of plants; she wanted all that she wanted—climbing roses, shrub roses, old roses, fragrant roses, hydrangeas, butterfly bush, viburnums, phlox, delphiniums, the lot. An arch links two sections of planter in the center, and on it grow several climbing roses and clematis, plus evergreen English ivy for winter interest. It is an enchanting garden to be sure, fragrant, flowery, full of pastel shades and billowy plants.

The sweetly scented cottage garden swollen with bloom is a romantic idea, the dream of many. Where cottage-style gardens occur in cities, they develop a following of admirers who walk or drive past them as often as possible. Whether pouring over a white picket fence or overflowing onto the sidewalk, these gardens are gifts to a neighborhood, and their gardeners are to be commended. Because cottage gardens focus so much on bloom, they have greatest impact in summer, when they give the joyous impression of a simple, carefree existence. But like the border, these are not low-maintenance gardens and require a gardener who enjoys puttering a little every day in summer, with major effort spring and fall.

In her small cottage-garden-in-the-city, Therese d'Monte tends hundreds of flowering plants to make joyous flower arrangements. Special treasures are plants whose seeds return annually from the compost to sow themselves.

border in a box

Audrey Litherland brings new meaning to the phrase container gardening. In raised boxes, eighteen inches high and twenty-four inches deep (forty-five by sixty centimetres) that edge her wooden deck, she grows many of her favorite flowering plants – glorious fragrant shrubs, vines, perennials, and roses, her passion. The boxes are bottomless, giving the shrubs a place to sink their roots eventually. Each spring, Audrey adds quantities of manure (sheep manure if she can get it), because many of these plants need lots of moisture and nutrients. (Manure and compost condition the soil so that it will hold moisture and make the nutrients available to roots.) The tall plants provide the sense of enclosure and privacy so necessary in the city. A bonus: plenty of flowers to make beautiful bouquets as often as she wants.

Love-in-a-mist (*Nigella damascena*), feverfew (*Tanacetum parthenium*), and lady's mantle (*Alchemilla mollis*) may enrich a bouquet with their tiny flowers, or the feathery foliage of fennel (*Foeniculum vulgare*), may accompany showier blooms.

Therese believes anybody can have a flower arranger's garden without elaborate training or a big budget. Every plant is a potential contributor, whether for a posy to sit on the kitchen window ledge, a hostess bouquet arranged and tied with raffia or iris leaves, vase-ready, or a large arrangement for a special event. She uses flowers, leaves, berries, seed heads, catkins, and shapely twigs or stems, foraging through the garden twelve months of the year. In winter, she seeks coniferous evergreens of every hue and broad-leafed evergreens such as *Euonymus fortunei.* In spring, many flowering shrubs need pruning, and these branches too may be enjoyed indoors. Even buttercups from the lane may grace an arrangement.

Many of the old-fashioned cottage plants seed themselves prolifically. This has several advantages but one drawback. If you beg a seedling or a few seeds of, say, sweet rocket (*Hesperis matronalis*), two years later you'll have an

Great vines

Vines are rewarding in any garden, but they are especially important in small gardens where ground space is at a premium. Roses, clematis, and ivy are the most popular, and there are many worthwhile varieties. Clare Philips suggests the following favorite vines suitable for small- to medium-sized gardens.

- *Akebia quinata* (chocolate vine). Perennial vine with semi-evergreen, rounded leaves and purple flowers with a spicy scent. Sun to partial shade.
- *Clematis.* Most are semi-woody, deciduous vines whose growth habits, flowers, and pruning needs vary widely. Scores are available in spring, and some of the best are *C. alpina* 'Frances Rivis', *C. macropetala* 'Markham's Pink', 'General Sikorsky', 'Gravetye Beauty', 'Jackmanii', 'Niobe', *C. paniculata,* 'Perle d'Azur', and *C. vitacella* 'Venosa Violacea'.
- *Cobea scandens* (cup and saucer vine). Tender perennial grown as an annual. Dramatic cream to purple flowers. Full sun.
- *Humulus lupulus* 'Aureus' (golden hops). Vigorous perennial vine with golden yellow foliage.

Rosa 'Rambling Rector' eagerly climbs the trellis in designer Clare Philips' garden.

Sun to partial shade; leaf color best in sun.

- *Hydrangea petiolaris* (climbing hydrangea). Woody deciduous vine that clings to a support, such as a fence, wall, or the trunk of a very large tree. Lacy white flowers. Sun or shade.
- *Ipomoea purpurea, I. tricolor* (morning glory). Annual vine with purple or blue flowers. Sun.
- *Lathyrus odoratus* (sweet pea). Annual vine with fragrant flowers. Sun.
- *Lonicera japonica* 'Halliana' (honeysuckle). Vigorous, woody vines bearing fragrant, pale yellow flowers. *L. henryi* is evergreen with red-purple flowers. Sun to part shade.
- *Parthenocissus henryana* (Chinese Virginia creeper). Deciduous, woody climber turning bright red in autumn. Sun or shade.
- *Rosa* (rose). Some of the best fragrant climbing roses are 'Alister Stella Gray', 'Mme Isaac Pereire', 'New Dawn', and 'Rambling Rector'. Full sun.
- *Tropaeolum speciosum* (flame creeper). Perennial climbing nasturtium bearing brilliant scarlet flowers. Sun or part shade.

impressive drift of mauve or white sweet-scented flowers, for free. There is something delightful about plants that pop up unbidden in sidewalk cracks or between stepping-stones. However, these fecund plants never know when to stop. Five foxgloves this year, fifty in two years' time. (They are biennial, that is, they grow from seed to flower in two years.) The neighbors will have them, welcome or not. It is useful to develop an ability to recognize self-sown seedlings when they first appear so their spread can be controlled, the young ones transplanted and grouped for effect rather than scattered everywhere. Words of caution, however, are easily disregarded. I was certainly deaf to warnings about Welsh poppy (*Meconopsis cambrica*) when I transplanted some from my sister's garden. Now I will be blessed with their cheery orange and yellow faces forever.

Propping up or staking weak-stemmed plants is necessary to prevent the taller plants from smothering the lower ones. The trick is to hold them up so invisibly, they appear to be self-supporting. Phoebe Noble's innovative method is to snip a piece of two-inch- (five-centimetre-) wire grid large enough to cover the plant, and lay it over top when growth begins in earnest. As stems and leaves reach through the grid, they are held together so individual stems do not flop. The wire can be gently pulled up the stems as the plant grows taller. If by summer a stake is needed, she pounds a length of reinforcing bar (rebar) into the ground at a corner of the grid. Rebar disturbs

Soften the edges

For flowering plants to soften the edge of a path, the front of the border or the top of a wall, choose low spreading plants or ones that flop gracefully forward.

- *Alchemilla mollis* (lady's mantle)
- *Euphorbia myrsinites* (donkeytail spurge)
- *Geranium* × *cantabrigiense* or *G. endressii* (cranesbill or hardy geranium)
- *Helianthemum nummularium* (sunrose)
- *Lysimachia nummularia* 'Aurea' (golden creeping jenny)
- *Nemophila maculata* (five-spot)
- *Nepeta* × *faassenii* (catmint)
- *Sedum reflexum, S.* 'Bertram Anderson', *S. spathulifolium*

Several kinds of poppy seed themselves rampantly, especially corn poppies (*Papaver rhoeas*), opium poppies (*Papaver somnifera*), California poppies (*Eschscholzia californica*), and Welsh poppies (*Meconopsis cambrica*). In her beachside garden, Linda Gravelin wanted a small sea of bright flowers able to thrive without watering, and with effort confined to several days per year. Over two years, these brilliant corn poppies have become the basis of a joyful and relatively low-maintenance summer garden.

For wildflower seed mixes to be successful, you must prepare the ground by removing grasses and any other plants that might compete. Often one or two plants from the mix will dominate, and if grasses were included (as is natural in a prairie meadow), they may crowd out most of the flowering plants. Ongoing weeding is essential or the meadow will soon be reclaimed by opportunistic local plants.

roots less, is stronger, and lasts longer than a wooden stake, and both grid and rebar are practically invisible.

By deadheading, that is, removing the flowers as they fade, you encourage a plant to produce more flowers. (Remember, the goal of the plant is to procreate, and if it does not produce seeds with one blossom, it tries again and again.) In some cases, the seed pod is almost as lovely as the flower. Pods of opium poppy (*Papaver somniferum*) are an asset all summer and dry easily for use indoors, and the hips of rugosa roses are brilliant from late summer until

The pickets, roses, delphiniums, and corn poppies are uplifting to many who pass by this old-fashioned garden. Using mostly flowers commonly grown in the 1920s, when their house was built, owners Brenda Peterson and Basil Stuart-Stubbs have re-created the optimism of that age. The garden's fragrant flowers include the pale pink rose 'Felicia'.

It is the perfect garden for hosting a summer party where neighbors wear white, drink gin, and bring their entries for the largest, longest-stemmed, most redolent sweet peas, jovially competing for the Grand Prix de Sweet Pea.

winter. This means you must choose more flowers, a set of seeds, or a compromise, deadheading some flowers and allowing others to ripen their fruit. Plants that bear clouds of tiny flowers are impossible to deadhead bloom by bloom. Hardy geraniums, for instance, are best clipped back hard to encourage both new flowers and fresh leaves. Plants with one great flush of bloom, such as delphiniums, can be cut right back to ground level after blooming, and they will send up new leaves and flower stalks for a second and occasionally a third flush.

Flowers for cutting were once planted in rows as part of the kitchen garden, but rarely so now. Most flower gardeners want their beds and borders to look like a glorious bouquet, so they plan to grow enough to leave in the garden and to cut for indoor use. If you want to make bouquets of elegant pale daffodils (*Narcissus* 'Dove Wings', for instance), you'll need to plant dozens. Frothy plants such as baby's breath, lady's mantle, and forget-me-nots are a great boon to flower arrangers as they combine well with many other larger blooms. Almost any flower can be grown for cutting, although some need special conditioning to preserve their freshness before they can be arranged.

For annuals or other plants from which you wish to save seed, you need to balance deadheading with seed-saving. One year I was fortunate to be given some very fragrant, old-fashioned sweet peas already sprouted. By snipping and clipping rigorously as the individual stems lost their flower petals and began to make pea pods, I was able to keep the plants thick and colorful all summer as they scrambled through a rose bush. In September, I began to leave some of the pods to mature. Once the pods were fat and brown and loosening their grip on the seeds, I harvested them for next year. With nasturtiums, I have the opposite policy: I try to collect and toss out as many of the seeds as I can, knowing there will still be far too many left to sprout next spring.

Alpine or rock gardens attract a special breed of devotees. Alpines are plants that originate above the tree line anywhere in the world, but most collectors include any very small plant, including dwarf trees and shrubs, minor bulbs, and the alpine flowers so beloved by hikers. These plants may languish in a regular bed or border because they have different requirements from other plants. On an alpine scree, the plants enjoy lean soil with sharp

Conditioning cut flowers

Flowers are mostly water, and wilt when they cannot replenish the water they lose. To make them last, cut flowers early or late in the day, then give them a long, deep drink of water – six to twenty-four hours – before arranging. Strip the lower leaves and remove any decaying debris so bacteria don't grow in the water.

Change the water daily if possible, and add cut flower food.

Blooms that last a long time in the garden will do the same indoors, but some need special treatment to stay fresh. For instance, to help plants with wide, hollow stems stand upright (such as foxgloves, lupins, and delphiniums), fill the stems with water and plug them with cotton batting. Nip off the unopened buds at the tip of the stalk. Other tricks include splitting woody stems of flowering shrubs, cauterizing stems that drip white sap (such as poppies) over a flame, or wrapping wilting roses in wet newspaper. Consult a flower-arranging resource book for the best methods for the plants you grow.

drainage, cool roots, and little competition from other plants. In a rockery, large, sometimes car-sized boulders are half buried or stacked to create numerous planting pockets and microclimates to accommodate plants needing extra warmth, or extra shade, or fissures in which to sink their roots. Alpinists, like other specialists, are an information-hungry group of gardeners; they want to know where and how each plant grows in the wild. Often the easiest way to coax an alpine into bloom is to grow it in a pot, where the conditions can be better manipulated.

The large rectangular stone troughs often used for growing alpines in England are rare here, but porous tufa rocks are available, and homemade troughs of reinforced cement and peat moss concrete, known as hypertufa, are popular and convincing alternatives. The pores of either tufa or hypertufa

Off-season flowering favorites

Anyone can have a feast of flowers in June. But to have plants you love coming into bloom or bearing berries all year is a worthy challenge.

Here are some of my flowering favorites for late fall through early spring. Making a list of your own favorites is a useful and pleasant exercise, bound to tell you something about what matters to you in the garden.

In fall, silver-leafed artemisias radiate with the glow of moisture on their surfaces, tall sprays of grasses reach statuesque proportions, and the seed heads of clematis shine like silk threads. Cape fuchsias (*Phygelius*), hardy *Fuchsia magellanica,* and tender *Salvia buchananii* have bloomed since early summer, and *Rosa* 'Bonica' has a second flush that will continue, with luck, until Christmas. Large-flowered *Colchicum autumnale,* pink *Nerine bowdenii,* and tiny autumn crocus species are fall-blooming bulbs that always take me by surprise. *Schizostylis coccinea* blooms from late August until severe frost, and multiplies quickly. *Cyclamen hederifolium* has exquisitely marbled foliage and perky pink to magenta flowers. *Osteospermum* is a tender perennial, but its mauve daisies thrive in cool autumn sunshine, and it usually produces buds that will open indoors until the plant is killed by true winter weather. The lilac berries of beautyberry (*Callicarpa bodinieri*), red or orange berries of cotoneasters and pyracanthas, orange *Iris foetidissima* seeds, fat white or pink clusters of *Pernettya mucronata,* and metallic blue berries of *Viburnum davidii* bring color and many birds to the autumn garden.

The winter garden, with a little forethought, can appear very animated. Red twigs of dogwood shrubs such as *Cornus alba* 'Elegantissima' or 'Spaethii' glisten in murky weather, and anything with yellow

Louise Dyer's spring border includes a mature corkscrew hazel (*Corylus avellana* 'Contorta'), Lenten rose (*Helleborus orientalis*), minor bulbs such as *Chionodoxa*, several primulas, and a fat cat.

or white variegated leaves – such as *Euonymus fortunei* 'Emerald 'n' Gold', *Carex morrowii* 'Variegata' or *Arum italicum* 'Pictum' – is an asset. Each brave flower is a treasure. *Helleborus foetidus,* the stinking hellebore (it doesn't) begins to open its buds in the darkest days, and by the end of January, *H. atrorubens* may have opened its first pretty buds. *Mahonia* × 'Charity' is a showier, winter-flowering cousin of native Oregon grape. After a messy summer, corkscrew hazel (*Corylus avellana* 'Contorta') bares its twisted branches and produces long yellow male catkins and nearly microscopic magenta female flowers. The witch hazels (*Hamamelis mollis* is very fragrant) perfume the air any time the sun warms their spidery blossoms. Several bulbs bloom in late winter, including *Crocus tommasinianus,* snowdrops (*Galanthus*), *Cyclamen coum,* and *Iris reticulata.*

When the winter aconites (*Eranthis hyemalis*) open their buttercup-yellow flowers and the first slugs appear, spring has begun to overtake winter. *Corylopsis pauciflora* (winter hazel) is one of many fragrant shrubs flowering from winter into spring.

The smaller daffodils, such as *Narcissus* 'Tête à Tête', 'Dove Wings', and 'Minnow', open much earlier than the larger ones, as do many of the species tulips, such as *Tulipa kaufmanniana,* or *T. saxatilis.* Bulbs marked as naturalizers will increase in number without lifting.

Hacquetia epipactis is an odd little perennial; it forms a low clump of fresh yellow-green flowers in earliest spring. *Anemone blanda* is another low-growing beauty best planted en masse under deciduous shrubs so it gets sun in winter and spring, but protective shade in summer.

As the weather warms, the pace of bloom quickens, and the special treasures begin to get lost in Spring's largess.

absorb moisture, keeping plant roots cool even in sun. Flat rocks placed vertically in gritty soil mimic narrow crevices and are perfect root runs. Primulas, saxifrages, and succulent sedums and sempervivums are good starters for a trough garden, but there are thousands of choices. More unusual ones can be grown from seeds ordered from the Alpine Garden Club of British Columbia or the Rock Garden Society of America. Some people join the societies just for the seed exchange, then find themselves drawn to the informative workshops, newsletters, plant sales, and pot shows, in which members compete for the prestige of Best Alpine in Flower, Best Cushion Plant, or Best Trough Garden. Tiny plants and miniature gardens have vast appeal.

We have local chapters of societies dedicated to growing dahlias, chrysanthemums, fuchsias and begonias, pelargoniums and geraniums, daylilies, rhododendrons, primulas, lilies, irises and, of course, roses. If a specific plant takes your fancy, you may find yourself becoming a collector. You'll seek out the picture books and the learned tomes on the subject, join a society and find kindred spirits. You'll acquire more and more species in your favored genus, more cultivars within each species and, sooner rather than later, you'll begin to rid yourself of garden extras such as lawn. Will your garden be a stiff collection of individual plants in one category or a welcoming

Forcing branches into bloom

In January or February, I like to hurry spring along by cutting branches of flowering shrubs such as magnolia, forsythia, or cherry, bringing them indoors to bloom a month or so early. If you have an under-utilized guest bathroom, use it as a miniature hothouse. To allow sap to flow, cut the end of each twig at a sharp angle or make vertical cuts with secateurs. The toilet bowl or tank makes a good holding reservoir; just add liquid or powdered cut-flower food. Turn up the heat a little, and shut the door. Or use a bucket of water, enclosing twigs in clear plastic to raise the humidity.

Check back every few days until the buds swell to bursting, when you can retrim branches and bring them out to enjoy. To make them last longer once they begin to open, put them in water outside by a glass door, by the front entrance, or on a table by a window where you can see them from indoors.

Happy in its hypertufa container, *Primula marginata* enjoys growing conditions that simulate its original home in the European Alps.

oasis unified by your passion for a single genus? Good garden design will make the difference, and show the special plants in the fullest possible range of use.

A walk in the garden—it's an idea that for many conjures up a leisurely picture of sunshine, soft summer breezes, and a galaxy of blooms. A great quantity of flowers can make a huge impact, especially if some hug the ground, some tower above, and they are at every level between. But in such a grand show, not every flower can be a star. Gardens where each bloom competes for attention with every other are unsettling. As in an opera, there might be places where the pace quickens with a chorus of roses, where there

Tiny-flowered plants such as hardy geraniums, feverfew (*Tanacetum parthenium*), and rose campion (*Lychnis coronaria*) fill this bed with color, complementing rather than competing with the lily (*Lilium regale*) in the garden of Joan and Joel Brink.

is room to go more slowly past islands of green or silver foliage, and places of high drama, where an unusual or large or brilliant white flower marks a climax. Large, showy blooms need the support of many smaller ones, as well as complementary foliage, structure, and space. A tree peony in bloom is a prima donna; all else must be subservient.

In each segment of the garden it helps to have one main idea. We rarely begin our gardens in this way; they most often evolve over years, taking as much advantage of what plants are available and affordable as the artistic contribution each makes to the whole. After a time, the garden may be more crammed and cramped, a muddle that has lost its impact by having too much. But there is a wonderful moment in the life of a gardener when he or she can dig a perfectly good plant out of the ground because it no longer contributes.

This is the beginning of the rewarding process known pretentiously as garden editing. Have you ever in one go pulled out a thousand forget-me-nots (notorious self-sowers) and had a sudden clear vision of what they had hidden? The plant so valuable for filling empty spaces with clouds of pastel blue stars may have come to crowd or obscure the other plants. Or perhaps you've found that a few cute plants bought in small pots have threatened to become uncontrollable monsters? I recall a droopy, knee-high, western hemlock that seemed to grow overnight like Jack's magic beanstalk to look down at the top of the roof; it fully intended to reach its potential height of two hundred feet (sixty metres).

These are good times to ask yourself tough questions. What are the most

Birds and bees

Flowers, insects, and birds have a close interrelation based on pollen and nectar. Many of the extraordinary forms, colors, and markings on flowers are designed to attract bees, butterflies, and hummingbirds, tempting them with nutritious nectar, and in turn, enabling their pollen to be traded with other flowers. Victoria naturalist Calvor Palmateer has a passion for birds, especially the hummingbirds indigenous to the west coast. His treacherously steep garden caters to them by providing a steady supply of nectar-rich flowers, some natives, but many wildly colorful exotics from the southern hemisphere.

Here are some ways to welcome hummingbirds and other birds to the garden.

- For a constant supply of nectar, use plants that bloom consecutively over a long period. Currant (*Ribes sanguineum, R. odoratum, R. lobbii*), *Phygelius,* perennial lobelias and salvias, red-hot poker (*Kniphofia* species), crocosmia, tender and hardy fuchsias, and penstemons are especially attractive to hummingbirds. Single-flowered varieties are preferable to doubles.
- Plant shrubs and trees for perching and taking cover. Keep a rough thicket in part of the garden. In fall, delay removing the dying tops of perennials, especially if they have seeds to contribute.
- Provide water in a pond, creek, or large birdbath. The sound of dripping water brings birds.
- Offer birdseed and suet all year. When birds are raising their nestlings, they need extra calories.

A sunflower opening according to its own pattern and schedule – a minor miracle.

important aspects of my garden? What effect am I trying to achieve? Dazzle? Calm? Detail? Sweep? Which elements of the garden impede this effect, and which contribute?

While your wants and needs gradually change, the garden matures. Trees cast more shade, groundcovers run amok, shrubs grow wider than expected. A garden may need several major overhauls over the course of its life, but each may be more exciting than the last. Sun-loving annuals may be replaced by flowering shrubs tolerant of partial shade. Common species may be sacrificed for the rare, the collectible. A plant you thought was the height of perfection four years ago seems hackneyed now. A reliable bloomer such as perennial *Lavatera* 'Barnsley' that goes from early summer until late fall may fade from favor, to be succeeded by something like the strange pineapple lily (*Eucomis bicolor*) or peanut-scented *Melianthus major,* offering dramatic forms, less cheery and colorful but perhaps more intriguing.

Our own horticultural biases strengthen with time—*yes* to red, *no* to pink (or vice versa), *yes* to gravel, *no* to bark mulch, *out* with amoeba-shaped beds, *in* with geometry. We go through stages of hating and loving botanical names. We want to acquire every possible plant, then say, No more just now. And so with our choices of flowering plants. Some turn out to be mere acquaintances, edited out, given away. But some of the plants we crave early on will always be cherished, for who can tire of an old true friend? These may be plants with loving associations—Johnny jump-ups (*Viola tricolor*) first encountered in Grandma's garden, the strongly scented rose 'Roseraie de l'Haÿ' grown from a cutting given by a favorite neighbor, the foxgloves (*Digitalis purpurea*) descended from seeds collected with your own children on a family vacation. I hope that as I gain knowledge of and an ability to grow trickier plants with a cachet of sophistication, I never lose my attachments to the simpler pleasures of the flower garden.

Food for Body and Soul

For many, gardening has become synonymous with growing ornamental plants, but the interdependence of people and plants began with cultivation for food and clothing. When we grow for our own food and drink, our healing medicines, our dyes, wreaths, and other cultural expressions, we link ourselves to every civilization in every time and place. From a pot of chives on the window ledge to a rambling family vegetable patch, from a single container of strawberries to an entire orchard or vineyard, we can grow useful plants in myriad ways.

Edible plants may be useful, but they are not so utilitarian as to be the sensible shoes of the gardening world. And despite the recent trend of viewing food as a list of fat grams and allergy warnings, food is about flavor, texture, fragrance, sensuality. A meal prepared with wholesome, home-grown ingredients is a celebration of life and an intimate connection with the earth. There are vegetables every bit as appealing to the senses as the showiest ornamental plant—stout, glaucous-leafed cabbages, fuzzy purple Japanese eggplants whose nearly black fruits have a waxen sheen, Swiss chard with veins that, when the sun shines through the leaves, glow fiery red. And the herbs! Hot pink whorls of bee balm with a scent that lifts the spirits, and prim green or dark maroon leaves of basil whose aroma arouses all appetites. But more than any other sense, we grow edibles for the pleasure of taste.

The flavor season begins with the first explosive mouthful of rhubarb or radish, builds through the early salads and strawberries, reaches a frenzied

OPPOSITE:
Rhubarb and chives alternate in handsome rhythm in the Vancouver Island garden of Sandra Holloway.

ABOVE:
Cabbage and kale are two of the most beautiful vegetables you might grow, certainly decorative enough to be grown where their veins, the sheen of their glaucous leaves, and the rose-like shape of the heads can be admired.

Opposite:
This mild-tasting salad includes with its butter lettuces the soft yellow petals of David Austin rose 'Graham Thomas', perennial lavatera, and violas, one of the easiest and prettiest additions to the vegetable patch.

peak in late summer and fall as sweet pears and tart apples are harvested and canned (and menacing barrows full of bland zucchini are distributed to willing or unsuspecting neighbors), and slows until the last ever-bearing raspberry rolls on the tongue, when the season slides into late root crops and lettuce sowings dependent on providential weather.

The question is not, why do some people grow their own food, but why doesn't everyone? Lack of time and space are the most frequently cited reasons, and these can be serious limitations. However, gardeners who have experienced the superior taste, freshness, and nutrition of what they grow and have felt the pride of bringing their produce to share at the table would never want to give these up. So if they cannot make or tend a large vegetable garden, they find ways to make the task possible, often by growing small quantities of easy, pest-resistant varieties with time-saving methods that minimize their labor. More than any others, vegetable gardeners seek out tips, shortcuts, and sure-fire methods to streamline their operations, whether on an acreage, in a modest backyard plot, or in pots on a patio, deck, or balcony.

In the past decade, growing vegetables in containers has really come into its own as designers and creative gardeners recognize the ornamental values of food plants and seek them out as patio subjects. With our long season of mild weather, a single pot could produce mixed early salad greens (fresher and cheaper than those pretty baby greens sold like gold dust in fancy produce markets) until mid-May, followed by a colorful selection of edible annual flowers—borage or nasturtium sown soon after the lettuce—during the warm dry summer months. A late summer sowing of more cool-weather salad greens (such as tangy mesclun, a blend of seeds that may contain lettuce, arugula, endive, cress, and chicory) will carry the fresh season right through fall. Even the laziest of gardeners—like me—can stuff a few romaine and red leaf lettuce seedlings bought at the corner store into a cedar planter box. Cut-and-come-again herbs, such as parsley, sage, and chives, make interesting foliage plants in pots or hanging baskets. Many rural or island gardeners depend on hanging baskets to keep leafy crops out of the reach of marauding deer.

eat your mauves

Hollyhock Farm has a handsome teaching garden as well as an extremely productive kitchen garden. Included with the crops bound for the kitchen are many ornamental plants – food for the eyes, the nose, and the soul.

Popping in flowers at the ends of vegetable rows is a way of making the garden a place of welcome, contemplation, and inspiration. And many of the flowers are edible. Mallow flowers, including lavateras, marsh mallows, and hollyhocks; rose petals; and herb blossoms, such as pink chives, clear blue borage, yellow nasturtiums, and lavender, can contribute to both table bouquet and salad bowl. Even the buds of daylily are a crunchy addition.

More strongly flavored blossoms include nasturtium, chives, and pot marigold (*Calendula officinalis*). But this is an area where experimentation must have its limits: many flowers, both wild and cultivated, are harmful when eaten. Like mushrooms, some are excellent, many are inedible because of taste or texture, and some are poisonous.

Culinary herbs and salad greens pay homage to fresh, healthy foods in the pots on Maureen Lunn's kitchen patio.

When I grew up, a green salad consisted of iceberg lettuce, celery, and odorless, tasteless tomatoes, with radishes or green onions thrown in for a really special meal; not much else was available in grocery stores. In the surge of recent culinary exploration, new ingredients, flavors, and textures have changed the green salad into a bowl of many colors. Tart French sorrel, peppery arugula, cilantro, purslane, endive, even dandelion leaves, plus dozens of lettuces—romaine, butterhead, looseleaf, oak leaf, and of course iceberg—are all easy to grow in the Pacific Northwest's moist spring, early summer, and fall. Most years we suffer only a few weeks of the warm dry summer weather that causes lettuces to bolt, before cool evenings enable us to grow cool-weather crops again. Oriental greens with exotic names like pac choi (bok choy), shisu, and tah tsai are extending the flavor palette, and undoubtedly more will be available as the demand continues to burgeon, often inspired by fine dining experiences in both Asian and new west coast cuisines.

Nori Fletcher, head gardener at Hollyhock Farm, a holistic resort on B.C.'s Cortes Island, knows lettuce better than most people; her organic garden produces over a thousand heads for the dining room each year. She plants successive crops every two weeks, sowing into seed trays, then transplanting into straw-covered vegetable beds as soon as the soil is workable in spring, and whenever there is room in the garden as other vegetables are harvested through summer and fall. As the soil is exceptionally sandy, nutrients are quickly leached out by rain or watering. To produce healthy, vigorous plants full of flavor, she treats her soil to organic additives, including well-rotted manure, slow-acting dolomite lime, wood ash, seaweed, and so-called green manure, a crop such as crimson clover or fava beans sown in fall for growth over the winter, then turned back into the soil in spring. Huge compost bins convert garden and kitchen waste into compost that feeds and improves the texture of soil, allowing it to hold moisture longer and enabling plant roots

Cream of the lettuce crop

Seed catalogs offer so many varieties of lettuce, it helps to have personal recommendations from someone in the know. Nori Fletcher of Hollyhock Farm grows more than a dozen different kinds, but after years of experimentation the ones listed below have given her the greatest success. Most are rarely offered for sale in produce departments.

- 'Romulus' is a romaine type.
- 'Red Sails' is a red looseleaf.
- 'Continuity', one of the tastiest and largest butterheads, is great for late spring and early summer sowing, when many varieties are doomed to bolt and become bitter as they mature in the dry season. It's known also as 'Merveille de Quatre Saisons'. 'Summertime' and 'Hilde' are two others less likely to bolt.
- 'Salad Bowl' and 'Red Salad Bowl' are a pair of frilled looseleaf lettuces large enough to be harvested by cutting the outer leaves and leaving the inner ones to continue developing; they are also good for repeat sowings throughout the growing season.
- 'Black-seeded Simpson' is an old looseleaf variety of palest lime green, best sown in early spring or fall.

Nori recommends that gardeners experiment with many varieties, keeping records of date sown, seed source, first and last harvest, quality of crop, and of course, flavor impressions. She keeps a detailed journal of all crops and major garden chores, but even notes scribbled on the inside of an opened seed pack may yield information valuable for making next year's plans.

Birds swoop from the tall hedges surrounding Sandra Holloway's vegetable garden to light on tripods supporting bean vines; a blizzard of butterflies flits from one leek flower to the next; on the surface of the thick straw mulch that blankets the soil, tiny black spiders scurry in every direction. This garden is a lesson in working in partnership with nature.

to take up nutrients more readily. Nori has studied organic gardening all her adult life, adding to her knowledge every year by reading, talking to other organic gardeners, and trying new methods and plants each year. In her home garden near Hollyhock, she feels free to experiment even more broadly. There she has recently tried using phosphorus-rich chicken manure applied "hot," that is, not yet completely rotted, in winter. It is usually recommended that manure only be applied to soil after a year of breaking down to prevent burning the plants with too much nitrogen. But she has produced outrageous-sized vegetables and flowers; her raspberry canes are twelve feet (over three metres) high and loaded with fat juicy berries.

Large gardens are well suited to an organic method of growing where a thick layer of straw mulch covers the soil. One Vancouver Island gardener inspired to use deep mulch is Sandra Holloway. Although a city apartment dweller, she tends a third of an acre (.13 hectares) in the countryside. With only one day each week to work in the garden, she needed to find the most efficient methods for starting plants, growing, and harvesting. Without straw and wood chip mulches, such a large garden would not be feasible for one woman to tend in such limited time. The eight-inch-deep (twenty-centimetre) mulch means she seldom needs to water: rain percolates through the mulch into the soil with very little evaporation. The oldest straw at the bottom of the mulch gradually breaks down to improve the condition and fertility of the soil, fostering the beneficial micro-organisms that live near the surface. This is unlike traditional (and more labor-intensive) methods of deep digging, turning the soil and loosening it with a spade or rototiller, which disturbs and kills many of these micro-organisms. Sandra keeps straw bales at hand, and just keeps adding to the top. A healthy community of tiny black spiders, snakes, and birds assists in controlling slugs and other pests so Sandra never resorts

A barrowful of squash

Squash is one of the most colorful, flavorful, and varied crops for hearty fall and winter eating. Sandra Holloway's bountiful selection begins with seeds germinated in cut-off milk cartons or special soil blocks on a sunny window ledge. As soon as the ground begins to warm in early May she transplants the seedlings into a permanent bed (she has not found crop rotation necessary with squash) mulched with wood chips – any type except cedar. If weather is cool, she places a large, sawed-off, plastic milk jug over each plant like a miniature greenhouse until the plant outgrows it.

During the summer, the sturdy vines creep in all directions, feeding heavily on fertile, compost-enriched soil; the squashes are unblemished as they develop on their clean bed of chips. Here are some of Sandra's all-time favorite varieties.

- 'Sweet Keeper'. Gray-green mid-size.
- 'Ambercup'. Small, round, deep orange.
- 'Blue Hubbard'. Very large, gray-green.
- 'Sweet Mama'. Dark green, roundish.
- 'Turk's Turban'. Large mottled orange with a distinctive turban shape perfect for a table center-piece.

OPPOSITE:
Raised beds are as attractive as they are beneficial to the vegetable garden of Karin Tigges.

to pesticides. After two or three years of mulch use, weeding becomes a minor task; weed seeds have a tough time germinating on the straw, so Sandra can spend her precious garden time planning, planting, and harvesting rather than hoeing, spraying, or sprinkling. To transplant a seedling germinated indoors, she parts the straw to expose a tiny area of the moist, friable soil beneath, adding compost only to the rectangle or row where it is needed. To make a direct sowing of seeds, she lifts the straw from a rectangular patch wherever there is space, sows, then places a covering of chicken wire over top to keep out cats. You can walk anywhere on the straw without worry of compacting the soil, kneel on its spongy surface without knee pads, and if you run short of time and can't stake your tomatoes, as Sandra did one entire season, you can let the plants sprawl over the clean straw. When a crop is harvested and the space not yet needed for another, fresh straw can be sprinkled over top, and in seconds the area looks tidy enough for visitors.

In the large area she devotes to growing squash, a mulch of wood chips—a firmer, drier medium for nestling the sometimes huge fruits—takes the place of straw. In winter, both the straw and wood chip areas require a dressing of urea, not technically an organic additive, but one very high in nitrogen, which is used up by the gradual breakdown of the mulches. Otherwise, this is an entirely organic food garden, where good soil care leads to strong, healthy plants that have natural disease- and pest-resistance. Physical barriers, such as the chicken wire, cloches, and other protective covers, also help avoid problems. When an infestation or problem does arise, there is enough variety and abundance within the garden to allow Sandra to shrug off any loss.

In smaller gardens, bales of straw may be impractical. The use of permanent raised beds is the method most favored by city farmers to achieve the same healthy soil as with deep mulch. Typically these beds are a maximum of four feet (1 metre) wide (so you can reach comfortably into the middle from either side) and raised anywhere from ankle to knee height. Soil in raised beds warms up earlier in spring, drains well, and because all foot traffic is in permanent paths between beds, stays uncompacted for good root development.

raised beds

In her new vegetable plot, approximately thirty-two by thirty-six feet (ten by eleven metres), Karin Tigges decided she wanted raised beds for the ease of cultivating the soil, and to get the benefits of good drainage and warm soil in spring and fall. To contain the beds, she used random rocks that were plentiful from clearing the land for this and other parts of the garden.

On the pathways she used a mulch of bark to discourage weeds. Because rock and bark mulch are materials natural to this coastal landscape, they were instantly at home. Her garden is plagued by the hungry roots of huge western red cedars, so each year she adds manure, homemade compost and seaweed gathered nearby.

Gradually the soil level will rise, giving more room for plant roots. To increase the productivity of her small space, Karin has planted espaliered apple and peach trees along one edge of the vegetable garden.

To dry twigs into arches, useful for low bush beans or to support a Reemay cloche, cut them while they are still flexible in early fall, and store them with the ends in two drain tiles spaced as desired. Next spring, they will hold their shape. Here Pam Frost uses grape vine arches to support bush beans.

The earth may be contained in wooden boxes, edged with stones, or simply mounded in place. If the bed is raised higher, it can be tended from a lawn chair or wheelchair. If the wall is capped with a broad board, it functions as a bench to kneel or sit on. Raised beds are invaluable where soil is very poor (sandy, stony, or heavy clay, for example), if it is too soggy, or if the land is sloped, causing soil and nutrients to wash downhill. Soil conditioners, such as manure, compost, or seaweed, stay in place and aren't squandered on paths. Mulch is still important on raised beds to suppress weeds and slow evaporation.

Depending on the materials used and the layout, raised beds may be highly decorative, and the small-space gardener is not so loath to devote the choicest sunny location to food production. Even a new vegetable patch can have a satisfying geometric or gracefully curved shape.

Plants that need support—pole beans, climbing peas, kiwis, tomatoes—challenge gardeners to find strong, efficient, economical, and often attractive means to keep things up in the light and air where they belong. Teepees great and small, sweeping zigzags of sturdy twine stretched between bamboo poles, hoops made from bent twigs, combinations of wire mesh, rebar, even flexible plastic pipe do stand-up duty and with a little flare, make the veggie patch look like performance art.

The smaller the garden the more important it is to integrate food plants with ornamental ones and with seating areas. Espalier or cordon fruit trees and climbing vegetables take up little space if planted against a wall. Fragrant herbs are doubly enjoyable pushing against the legs of a sun-drenched bench; their aromas are released each time their leaves are disturbed, and their leaves and flowers soften paved areas. Colorful leaf lettuces, ferny-topped carrots and many other vegetables have foliage attractive enough to be tucked into the front of a flower border.

On a high-rise balcony, hanging baskets can host snap peas or bush beans, even cucumbers. Moss baskets are great for tucking in lettuce, culinary herbs, and cheery nasturtiums. Pole beans such as scarlet runners quickly rise to make an edible privacy screen. The keys to success are containers of generous proportions, moisture-retentive soil, weak weekly liquid feedings, and frequent watering or a drip irrigation system on a timer as vegetables may be bitter if the plants are stressed by drying out.

Most food crops need plenty of available moisture and nutrients, and one of the best means of providing them is the all-important compost, the secret pride of almost every kitchen gardener. Making healthy compost is like

Incredible edibles

Landscaper Jennifer Jones encourages her clients to include food-bearing plants in the landscape. Twining vegetables – runner beans, cucumbers, zucchinis – grown over an attractive support make a focal point in the garden. Rhubarb, she says, is wasted in the vegetable patch, and can be used in a sunny border where its handsome leaves function as hostas do in shade. Grapes and kiwis require more planning, as they need very sturdy supports and plenty of room. Grown over an arbor, they can form the roof of a cool patio.

Many dwarf fruit tree varieties are suitable for home gardens, including almond and fig. Apple trees are now available as step-over espaliers (the fruiting branches run parallel to the ground, only knee-high), and taller espaliers grafted with six different apple varieties are an orchard-in-a-tub.

practicing alchemy; when you pull the wormy, crumbly, forest-sweet Black Gold from the pile and remember the kitchen and garden detritus that went into it, you know you have harnessed one of the great natural forces. A compost bin (or several) belongs in every kind of garden. Those who grow their own fruits, herbs, and vegetables are very conscious of the benefits of organic practices. Compost, like animal manures, conditions the soil; that is, it improves the moisture-retaining structure of the soil, even in well-drained sites, so plant roots can draw up the minerals and other nutrients that are dissolved in the water. Compost contributes many nutrients as well as a host of necessary micro-organisms. Other important organic soil conditioners include bone and blood meal, kelp meal, fish meal, and rock phosphate.

There are many commercial composters on the market, and just as many good ways to make your own. Most municipalities encourage composting, but local regulations may restrict the type of bin. Conventional wisdom calls for a compost pile composed of alternating layers of fresh green and dried

Recipe: compost box lasagna

For an efficient, sweet-smelling compost in a wood and wire mesh box or a wire mesh cylinder approximately one yard (one metre) in dimension.

1. Loosen the soil at the base of the box with a fork.
2. Place a thin layer of twigs at the bottom to foster air flow.
3. Add a three-inch (eight-centimetre) layer of Brown Stuff – dried leaves, straw, newspaper strips, sawdust.
4. Add a three-inch (eight-centimetre) layer of Green Stuff – kitchen vegetable waste (no animal products or fats), and stems and leaves from the garden diced as finely as sanity allows.
5. Sprinkle a thin layer of garden soil. This is the starter, like yeast in bread, containing microbes that will do the cooking.
6. Repeat steps 3, 4, and 5 (the more variety, the better) until the pile is as high as it is wide, usually a cubic yard (cubic metre) or so.
7. If the weather is very dry, add a little water.
8. Wait and stir. For quick compost, stir the pile every week or two, any time you should be vacuuming. For patient compost, stir it up only if you really feel like it.

Freeform compost

Instead of using a box, dig a shallow pit, and week by week add kitchen scraps in a little hole in the center with a layer of Brown and Green Stuff as above, always adding a little garden soil too. Turn as above. Be especially selective with kitchen

Pretty enough for the front of the border? Japanese eggplant shares a sunny southern portion of the author's ornamental foliage border.

scraps, though; even fruit or grains may attract critters.

Seafood compost

Add some thin layers of seaweed. Excellent for potassium and many trace minerals.

Compost piquante

Add a layer of moist manure. This really heats up a cool compost.

California compost

Throw in watermelon rinds. The microbes will love you.

Hurry-up compost

Add urine to kick-start the process. (No kidding; it's high in nitrogen.) Or add worms. Usually the red wiggler worms that thrive in composts arrive unaided. But if they don't, beg a bucketful of wormy compost from a friend, or find a pile of rotting leaves, and add some mushy leaf mold to the center of the pile.

Compost grande

If you haven't enough Brown and Green, add layers of chips from a chipper-shredder. Commercial tree trimming firms are usually glad to give some up. Ask what's in the mix, and avoid cedar chips.

Other flavors

Try crushed eggshells, paper products such as coffee filters or paper napkins, and grass clippings in very thin layers or very well mixed in. Just be wary of any poison-ridden items, as the chemicals in them may well survive the composting process.

Grapes ripen in September's sun for October's harvest.

brown materials with garden soil. Any pile of vegetative matter breaks down given enough time, but most gardeners want to turn today's raw materials into usable compost in less than a year. The energetic fork over their piles, aerate with ski poles, bamboo, or pipes, fluff the stuff with a fork, and speed the whole process up so it finishes in under two months.

While many gardeners like to dabble in everything—a few herbs, some tomato plants, maybe a berry patch as well as a variety of trees, shrubs, and ornamentals—some food gardeners burn with the specialist's passion. It takes a different level of commitment, knowledge and, often, space to grow an orchard of fruit or nut trees, to research a garden dedicated to Shakespearean herbs, or to experiment with as many beans as possible.

The west coast is not known for fine wines, yet Ken Cambon took that as a challenge rather than a taboo when he decided to plant a vineyard on a sunny slope overlooking Georgia Strait. He has put up with rainy springs with poor pollination, rainy summers that keep the sugar content low, rainy autumns that mold the fruit; hungry robins and really ravenous bears; friends who sometimes doubt the wisdom of the project. But for him, the process of learning about different kinds of grapes, methods of growing them, and wine-making techniques has been a journey with as much laughter and joy as frustration or discouragement. Each fall Ken and his wife, Eileen, invite family and neighbors to participate in the harvest, a chaotic day of racing children, darting dogs, the displaying of juice-stained hands, all ending with a hearty feast and samples of previous years' vintages. What other crop could inspire such merriment?

The antiquity of herbs and the participation in practices that connect us with gardeners of old is alluring. While many west coast gardeners balk at rigidly symmetric gardens, geometry and herbs seem to go together anywhere. There's magic in planning such a shapely planting as a simple circle or a complex knot garden, a garden in a square, a rectangle, or even a pentangle. A fragrant pathway where scent is as striking as visual beauty appeals to all the senses as well as to the intellect.

Herbs, always important to people who enjoy delicious food, are now undergoing a renaissance for their therapeutic and medicinal values after decades of decline caused by an increasing reliance on pharmaceutical drugs.

Herbs for healthy teas

What could be more joyous than snipping a tea of herbs picked fresh from the garden while the kettle comes to the boil? For most of the year herbal teas, also called infusions or tisanes, must be made from dried herbs, but during the growing season, the new leaves, stems, and flowers of many herbs can be used fresh. With homemade teas as with all other home-grown foods, you can ensure they are free of pesticides. Flavorful herbs have both nutritional and medicinal properties.

Herbalist Elaine Stevens recommends experimenting with combinations of the common herbs below, most grown also for cooking. Steep the leaves, seeds, or flowers for ten to fifteen minutes. Try one or two at a time to find the strength, flavors, and combinations that appeal.

- Peppermint and spearmint aid digestion after a meal and freshen the mouth. Peppermint should not be given to young children.
- Fennel or dill seeds and parsley leaves and stems are more savory; they are also excellent digestives, reducing gas and flatulence.
- Chamomile flowers, either German chamomile (*Matricaria recutita*) or Roman chamomile (*Chamaemelum nobile*), make a calming, slightly sedative tea.
- Lemon thyme, lemon grass, and lemon balm all have a citrus flavor and are tasty added to other teas.
- Lavender flowers, rosemary leaves, sage leaves, hyssop flowers and leaves, and borage leaves are also well worth sampling.

paths make scents

Oregano reaches forward to offer its fragrance to passers-by at Everlasting Summer, a dried flower and herb farm on Salt Spring Island.

It's not an aerobic way of walking, but a slow, aromatic sensation. Herbs are especially effective when planted between paving stones, leaning over the path or bulging at a bend in the route. Woolly and creeping thyme are perfect for ground level; lavender and bee balm are taller fragrant edgers, and pushing past the leaves of a rosemary bush at a sunny protected corner is good cause for breathing deeply. Add sweet-smelling old roses and oriental lilies, a buddleia bush or honeysuckle vine, and you can turn a short walk into an aroma therapy session.

Oregano's roots spread quickly, so you can make a fragrant and romantic allée inexpensively by splitting the plant each fall, and replanting some further along the path. Mint and lemon balm spread even more rampantly than oregano, so fast that they are best grown with their roots contained in pots or planters, or between a sidewalk and a wall.

Or how about a Pizza Walk? Lyn Noble delights her grandchildren with a dry sunny path where oregano, thyme, sage, and marjoram grow along the edges and in the gaps. When her grandchildren visit, they scamper along the path, brushing the leaves with their feet to release the aromas of pizza and spaghetti. And if homemade pizza is on the menu, they're eager to snip their favorite flavors.

The suspicion that grew against old-fashioned remedies in the face of scientific advances is often now aimed at drug companies, and people are eager to rediscover the traditional uses of herbs, tempered by a rapidly growing modern experience of what works.

Another ancient food enjoying a renewed following is the edible seed, including beans, barley, quinoa, wheat, and amaranth. On Salt Spring Island, Dan Jason began experimenting with seeds for their nutrition and taste. That led to seeking out and exchanging varieties both new and very old; forming a seed company, Salt Spring Seeds; and advocating through his writings such practices as seed saving and sustainable organic gardening—living in intimate harmony with the land. For beans that dry well for use in chili, salad, soup, or stew, Dan recommends varieties that mature early, in ninety to a hundred days. Three of his favorites are 'Ireland Creek Annie', 'Nez Percé', and 'Montezuma Red'.

Plants useful for crafts—dried arrangements, wreaths, twig furniture, and a wealth of other decorative works—fill a niche for some gardeners. Audrey Ostrom is fascinated by the many plants that can be used for the woven arts, including basketry (willow, wisteria, clematis, honeysuckle), spinning (yucca, phormium, milkweed, hemp, flax), and dyeing (dahlia, marigold, dyer's coreopsis, sumac, eucalyptus, madder). To dye her homespun wool in a range of exquisite natural colors, she collects fruit, flowers, tree bark, leaves, or roots. Arbutus bark, for example, gives deep golds and browns. Concord grapes impart a subtle palette of purply grays. Dahlia flowers of any color produce rich ambers and rusty oranges, depending on the mordant used to fix the dye. As with food crops, the process of growing, harvesting, then making practical use of plants extends the experience of gardening.

Like composing music or poetry, gardening may be workaday or inspirational, prosaic or profound. Growing useful plants need never be judged solely on cost effectiveness, efficiency, size of produce, or even superiority of taste. Gardening is such a fundamentally human activity and its practice so worthy, it needs no more justification than does singing a love song.

Opposite:
Oregano plants edge the path in the herb garden at Everlasting Summer.

No Space Is Too Small

The Pacific Northwest sometimes seems like the Land of Large—immense mountains, vast sea, towering trees—yet many of us garden in a small way, on city or suburban lots, townhouse patios or apartment balconies. The term "small garden" is slippery—to one it may be a single oversized pot intensely cultivated, to another anything less than a country estate. Yet even a large garden is a series of smaller segments, vignettes, ideas that may be equally—or more—suitable to the tiny garden. The more densely populated our situation becomes, the more important it is to have a private green space as a retreat.

There are many advantages to tending a small garden, so there's no need for acreage-envy. The tasks are so manageable. It takes ten minutes to hand prune a dwarf apple tree in a large patio pot (forget the ladder and telescoping pruning saw), and as you pass by, you can pick off pests before their numbers overwhelm. Seen up close, the apples are like Christmas tree baubles; with the time you save not mowing an orchard, you could polish each apple or tie a satin ribbon on each stem. Let a low-growing clematis, such as delicate blue *Clematis integrifolia,* scramble through the apple tree's branches and you can enjoy a more complex picture with greater seasonal interest in the same space. The smaller the garden, the more precious each plant becomes. There is great satisfaction in taking time to know each plant intimately, the pattern of its leaves, the progression of its buds, blossoms, and seed heads, its scent, its texture on the fingertips, the slow color changes through the seasons.

OPPOSITE:
On a north-facing apartment balcony, Brenda Scherbatty has made a complete garden by using every bit of the available forty-five square feet (four square metres). Concrete pavers, rocks, driftwood, lattice, moss, water, and feeders for birds, and plants in pots all contribute. Indoor plants enjoy the summer outdoors, and everything can be shifted to take best advantage of plants in flower. To overwinter hardy plants, Brenda clusters them close to the building, protecting pots with driftwood and burlap.

ABOVE:
The delicate growth habit of *Clematis integrifolia* makes it an ideal partner for a tiny tree.

Small-space gardening has its challenges, too. Just as each beautiful blossom counts more when seen up close, so does each eyesore. Utility poles and power lines, awkward buildings, the windows, doors, and sundecks next door often cause despair, and anyone living on a busy street knows how disturbing buses and cars—even parked ones—can be. Excluding or at least limiting these distractions is critical; if you can control what is visible from within the garden, it can be a restful haven. It may seem contradictory, but enclosing a small garden so that there are fewer outside influences makes it more usable and therefore seem more spacious in area and volume. A well-behaved evergreen hedge or a fence topped with a light pergola or lattice to support vines turns a public front yard into a garden for growing favorite plants, watching birds, or lingering over summer meals.

Of course, not all eyesores can be blocked by a hedge, and may need to be disguised instead. Painting a junky garage or work shed and facing it with wide-spaced lattice could transform it into the perfect backdrop for an elegant bench and climbing roses. A shapely tree carefully placed can make an unsightly power pole nearly disappear. To mask an ugly view, use something flamboyant in the foreground—an oversized ornamental grass that quivers in the slightest breeze or a raised urn spilling dazzling flowers—that will distract from the offending sight and hold attention within the garden.

But view control can be more than retaining desirable views and blocking out what is unwanted. The Japanese use a principle of borrowing scenery, designing the garden to play actively on the relationship of elements within the garden to natural elements beyond, especially neighborhood trees, mountains, sky, or sparkling sea. By leaving strategic gaps, by artistically pruning holes in the tree canopy, or by varying the height of a hedge to block buildings but not tree tops, you may pull the view into your garden. You can create an echo of a cherished sight by including a small version of it in the garden. A dwarf hemlock on a low mound in the garden repeats the concept of forest and mountain. A birdbath that reflects the sky represents the sky itself.

The perception of space can be altered by clever arrangement of paths and plants. A path that is wider at its outset, then narrows and curves behind a

Above:
A fragrant 'Mozart' rose is enhanced by the woven teepee that supports it in Jocelyn Horder's garden.

Opposite:
Marion Clarke's patio is both outdoor living room and extra-ordinary garden.

Marion Clarke, with the help of garden designers Michael Luco and James Bennett, enclosed her tiny patio, making it a private realm and a comfortable outdoor room in a bustling urban neighborhood. The vertical cedar slat fence lets light and air into the garden but blocks out most of the distractions of the street.

The whole garden is only about three hundred square feet (twenty-seven square metres), much of it surfaced in brick. A pergola covers about a third of the garden, further defining the space. It also supports deciduous clematis and wisteria vines that provide floral interest and shade in spring and summer, but let the light of winter penetrate. There is just enough tempered glass over one end of the pergola to protect furniture from rain; the table and bench stay outdoors year round.

Marion combines in-ground plantings of trees, shrubs, and shade-loving woodland perennials such as lady's slipper (*Cypripedium reginae*), bloodroot (*Sanguinaria canadensis*), and columbine (*Aquilegia* hybrids) with an eclectic mix of pleasing objects and pots that she rearranges through the season. Because the garden is visually an integral part of her home, the warmth of a brick-paved garden room is especially appropriate.

patio perfect

Clipped box (*Buxus sempervirens*) in rectangular pots are formal elements in the entrance to Susan Ryley's garden, but the shaggy shape of *Lonicera nitida* 'Baggesen's Gold' prevents rigidity.

fence or group of bamboo or shrubs, seems far longer than a path that goes straight to its destination at a uniform width. The same illusion can be produced by repeating key plants or colors along the edges of a path, but planting them at closer and closer intervals toward the far end. In a rectangular space, putting a path or patio along the diagonal axis gives greater depth.

Water, too, makes a small garden seem larger. Where the water is deep, dark, and still, it invites contemplation, halting the pressures of time. Reflected plants double in volume. By an entranceway, a potted sword fern overhanging a tall urn of water is a simple and elegant statement. Add a shapely rock, and the universe is at your doorstep—the oceans, the mountains, the forests, and the reflected heavens.

The sound of moving water masks or neutralizes outside noise. But before choosing a fountain, listen to a variety of types, paying attention to the effect the sound has on you. A trickle or drip that cools and soothes one psyche may torture another. Burbling, spraying, and tumbling waters each evoke specific psychological and even physiological responses. Choose carefully. (Wind chimes and gongs should also be tested before purchase. I adore the low foggy notes of large tubes or gongs, but many prefer the light tinkle of bells or glass chimes.)

Another strategy for making small spaces appear larger, one that garden designers often employ, is to block the view of the garden itself from within, so you do not see the whole space or its limitations at one time. This is the antithesis of the "spin-dryer" effect, where all plantings would be kept to the perimeter of the garden. By planting a small deciduous tree, such as a lace-leaf Japanese maple or a shore pine, in the middle of the space or in a bed that reaches into the middle from one side, you create two spaces, "here" and "over there." If the tree is kept pruned in an open habit, you can peek through it to the garden beyond, creating a sense of great depth that is absent

Trees for small gardens

When choosing a tree for a small garden, look for varieties that are very slow growing or dwarf. Try to picture how the tree will look in a decade or two. Consider overall size, shape, and leaf color, but also the qualities valued most in fall and winter, such as branch structure, bark texture, or berries.

- *Acer griseum* (paperbark maple)
- *Betula utilis* var. *jacquemontii* (Himalayan white birch)
- *Clerodendrum trichotomum* (glory-bower)
- *Cornus kousa* (Korean dogwood)
- *Cornus alternifolia* (pagoda dogwood)
- *Cotinus coggygria* 'Royal Purple' (purple smoke tree)
- *Hamamelis mollis* (witch hazel)
- *Juniperus scopulorum* 'Skyrocket' (Rocky Mountain juniper)
- *Juniperus chinensis* 'Aurea' (golden Chinese juniper)
- *Oxydendrum arboreum* (sourwood)
- *Parrotia persica* (Persian ironwood)
- *Prunus* 'Accolade' (flowering cherry)
- *Pyrus salicifolia* 'Pendula' (willow-leafed pear)
- *Sorbus hupehensis* 'Pink Pagoda' (mountain ash)
- *Styrax japonicus* (Japanese snowbell)
- *Taxus baccata* (yew)

in an unobstructed garden plan. To simulate the effect before making a change, block out the spaces with lawn chairs, ask family members holding umbrellas to stand in for trees, or make photocopies of garden photos and sketch in the possible plantings.

Seating areas are most inviting in a well-defined space. A small concrete or stone patio, wooden platform, or a tiny circular lawn would be comfortable surfaces for a table, chairs, or a lounge. Smoother surfaces, including wood and brick, need frequent cleaning to prevent algae growth that can be treacherous underfoot in our moist climate. In a garden where a panoramic view draws attention out past the garden, a low wall or knee-high boxwood hedge gives a seating area a greater sense of security. But equally important to the ground surfaces are the vertical elements. In addition to fences, walls, and hedges, consider completing a garden room with a pergola or a canopy of overhanging deciduous trees.

ABOVE:
Three bonsai trees, evergreen *Pinus densiflora* 'Pendula' and deciduous *Acer palmatum* and *Larix kaempferi* 'Pendula', echo the forms and colors of the autumn forest within Terry Welch's large garden.

OPPOSITE:
Teresa and Ken Rowley's garden is an urban oasis.

The possibilities for selecting plants are as diverse in a small garden as in a large one. More depends on the imagination and interests of the gardener than on the limitations of space. Some small-scale gardeners choose only small plants—dwarf evergreens, low-growing alpines, petite bulbs, and well-behaved perennials that won't soon outgrow their allotted spots. A more dramatic plan is to choose oversize perennials that rise from the ground in early spring, shoot steadily upward until their flowers look you in the eye, tower overhead by autumn, then turn brown and die theatrically. Other gardeners may choose a theme—a calm Japanese garden, a cool white-and-green garden, a food-producing family garden, a bird-friendly thicket, an eccentric tropical garden, or a scented rose garden. An enclosed space intensifies fragrance by trapping the air.

Containers extend the scope of any garden, regardless of its size. A collection of pots is a license to play. Perhaps this is the reason so many of us began our gardening careers by potting a few colorful annuals to brighten a balcony or front porch.

Pot gardens entice with their variability and impermanence; it is safer to plant flowers in a window box than choose a tree that may outlive us all.

geometric motifs

Every part contributes to this small garden, owned by Teresa and Ken Rowley and designed by Michael Luco. Still waters of the pond have a calming influence. Spiky-leafed iris makes an exciting counterpoint to the flat surfaces, including the water, and punctuates the fine-leafed plants. Blue-flowered *Agapanthus* in its fat round pot stands guard at the pond's corner, emphasizing the square formality with its curves. Straight sides echo other squares and rectangles in the garden – the sundial, the checkerboard paving, and low box hedges that surround currant bushes grown as standards.

Formal gardens can be lively and varied, so long as their symmetry is softened by unexpected or playful details. The square motif repeated throughout the garden unifies the design. Geometric motifs are often drawn from architectural details, but the primary shapes, the circle and square, have great presence and impact when used boldly.

The view of English Bay is breathtaking from the stone-paved terrace Thomas Hobbs and Brent Beattie made in their Vancouver garden. But the garden always competes successfully for attention with its richly textured, horticulturally sophisticated, often eccentric plantings and splendid architectural details. Rather than leaving the middle empty for a roomier space, they altered the scale with a huge antique iron urn and circular planter centrally placed. This gives the garden an illusion of greater size and depth. Because the whole terrace is not viewed at a glance and the borders are irregularly shaped, a visitor is never so aware of the limits of space as the delight of detail.

The exciting fan-shaped fronds of a hardy windmill palm (*Trachycarpus fortunei*) both mask and distract from what Tom calls his Chernobyl – a tangle of utility lines and a pole that would otherwise mar the view and detract from the garden. Two graceful weeping beeches assist in hiding the mess and contrast with the linear form of the palm.

In pots we can freely experiment with new color combinations and leaf forms, following a different theme each year, or season by season we may build a collection of pleasing pots and well-cared-for plants.

Except for the heaviest ones, pots can be shifted into new arrangements as plants come in and out of bloom. Because lilies have a short but spectacular bloom time, some gardeners keep them potted in an out-of-the-way spot until they are in bud, then move them to a place of honor to be fully enjoyed. As soon as the last lily blossom withers, the pot is hidden away again while the leaves continue to send energy to the bulb for next year's bloom.

Container gardens are not merely miniature gardens. Horticulturally, a pot provides very specific growing conditions, better for some plants than in the ground. Depending on the pot you choose (its volume, shape, and the material it is made of), the soil you put in it (either a standard potting mix or, for special plants such as alpines or cacti, one specially formulated for sharp drainage), and where you place the pot (sun, shade, or partial shade; exposed to wind or protected), you may be able to replicate the conditions of almost any climate and soil in the world. Plants that prefer confined roots and soil on the dry side, such as pelargoniums, thrive in terra cotta pots or wooden boxes.

If soil is very poor, as is often the case in new developments where fill has deeply buried the original soil, you could use pots to grow plants that would not survive otherwise. Plants that would overrun all the others in the ground, such as bamboo, mint, or variegated goutweed (the dreaded *Aegopodium podagraria* 'Variegatum'), can be safely grown in containers, as long as you watch for roots escaping from the drainage hole.

By raising some pots on plinths, either the refined ones now widely available in garden shops, or makeshifts of sturdy fence posts, logs, or inverted pots, you can create a three-dimensional, multiheight tableau. In small gardens, growing plants vertically, layer upon layer, is a key method of increasing growing space. Almost anything can support a vine: a trellis, a tree, a chain hanging from the eaves, a twig tripod, or a spiral sculpture purchased just for the purpose.

ABOVE:
***Echeveria* species, *Senecio rowleyanus*, glaucous *Mertensia simplicissima*, and *Origanum* 'Barbara Tingey' are an agreeable group in a pot by Thomas Hobbs and Brent Beattie.**

OPPOSITE:
Luxuriant plantings and a Mediterranean flare are hallmarks of Hobbs' and Beattie's garden.

OPPOSITE:
Judy Newton's leafy balcony is a cool, welcoming space.

Perennials, grasses, spring and summer bulbs, herbs and vegetables, vines, shrubs, and small trees are all potential container subjects. Even tender tropical plants enjoy a summer outdoors in our relatively cool summers, and their exotic foliage is like an unexpected spice in a stew.

By examining the light conditions your pots will enjoy (or endure), you can select appropriate plants. The entrance to my home is very dark and receives no rainfall—not a hospitable place for growing. I've planted a native groundcover, *Oxalis oregana,* in compost-enriched potting mix in small rectangular terra cotta pots along the railing. All the oxalis asks is a little water every week or two; in return it gives a dense, evergreen clump of shamrock-shaped leaves, and from time to time, tiny white flowers. It almost always looks tidy, and if the leaves get tatty after winter freezing, I snip them with scissors. For a windswept sunny spot, you might choose sturdy, compact, drought-tolerant plants—blue fescue or rugosa roses, for example.

The best fun, though, is not in choosing safe plants that will perform predictably, but in taking risks, experimenting with the possibilities for both plants and pots. The containers can contribute to style. Perhaps your garden is formal—think of a shapely clipped box in a classical urn raised on a pedestal. Maybe you prefer a romantic elegance, using billows of frothy pale blue annual lobelias, white pelargoniums, and tiny-leafed gray *Helichrysum petiolaris* in a cluster of Italian terra cotta pots. If you'd rather have a funky assortment, try off-the-wall plants like toothy agaves, oversized alliums, or fiery Japanese blood grass in anything-goes pots, from boots and buckets to brake drums. Once you decide to try containers and combinations that are new to you, you'll begin a collection with a style that is distinctly your own.

One of the most rewarding aspects of gardening in an age of rapid growth and development is the positive role we gardeners can play in urban and suburban settings. Foliage of trees, shrubs, and lawns cools the air in summer, increases the available moisture during drought, and traps airborne pollutants. Shrubs provide shelter and nesting places for the birds and insects that have been supplanted by urban sprawl. By learning about the habits of the creatures that belong here, we can improve their survival rates.

a shady balcony

A successful shade garden need not be grounded under a grove of trees. On her north-facing balcony garden, Judy Newton grows many of the plants you would expect in a grander garden – hostas, elegant ferns, lacy groundcovers, even a large shrub, *Fatsia japonica*. Most are in plastic pots, which do not dry out as fast as clay ones. To further the sense of "garden," she raises plants to different heights on wooden vegetable boxes or upturned pots, and making a multilayered composition. A surprise: Judy fills a black pond liner each spring for a naturalistic water feature. Its edges are disguised by the surrounding plants. In fall, she drains it using a siphon hose, and stores it on its side over the winter.

When planning a roof or balcony garden, consider the effects of weight and water on the building. The heaviest pots must be located where there is sufficient structural support; if in doubt, get professional advice. Equally important is developing a system of drainage so excess water does not pool or leak into apartments below.

The home garden may never be a good place for a cougar or coyote, but salamanders, frogs and newts, snakes and lizards, ground beetles, and increasingly rare butterflies can find good habitats if we are careful. The number of pest insects is tiny compared to the miraculous variety of garden-worthy ones, and many of the critters the garden supports eat the pests.

Barbara Flynn of Redmond, Washington, tells the story of the day bulldozing began for a large housing subdivision near her home. The fence enclosing her average-sized suburban garden, a miniature wildlife refuge, was lined with birds of many species, looking shell-shocked as their forest homes were suddenly demolished in favor of human habitation. Some of these fugitives found at least temporary shelter in Barbara's garden.

Birds, snakes, butterflies, bees, dragonflies, and ladybugs are a few of the creatures she welcomes by providing the basics—food, water, and shelter. Her pond is tiny and secluded, but a pump circulates the water, and the gentle splashing sound signals its presence to animals. Thick shrubs and vines and rougher areas that are seldom cultivated provide shelter and nesting sites. Several feeders and plants with berries or long-lasting seed pods are essential sources of year-round food. Above all, the garden is pesticide-free. There may be hope for the new subdivision homes: along Barbara's block, more and more neighbors have branched out from the lawn and bark mulch

Very tall perennials

Big plants have great impact in small spaces. But a word of warning: they need supervision, or they become menaces. Their roots may need containment so they don't take over the entire garden, and some will require tactful staking, usually in early summer.

- *Anchusa azurea* 'Loddon Royalist'
- *Eremurus robustus* (foxtail lily)
- *Eupatorium purpureum* (joe-pye weed)
- *Foeniculum vulgare* 'Purpureum' (bronze fennel)
- *Helenium* 'Moerheim Beauty' (Helen's flower; sneezeweed)
- *Helianthus* × *laetiflorus* (perennial sunflower)
- *Lilium* 'Casa Blanca' (Casa Blanca lily)
- *Macleaya microcarpa* (plume poppy)
- *Miscanthus sinensis*
- *Romneya coulteri* (California tree poppy)
- *Thalictrum delavayi* 'Hewitt's Double' (meadow rue)

Phormium tenax 'Purpureum' is one of a hundred potted treasures in Barbara Flynn's garden.

yard. They have begun, as many of us have, to plant for beauty while taking an active role in fostering a healthy environment in our own small spaces, restoring a little of the natural world.

If gardening is about making a private oasis, it is also about building community. Because gardeners spend so much time outdoors, they are likely to meet neighbors, children, dog-walkers, and delivery people. The rare day when I clean up my easy-care front garden is a sociable one. People coming home from work slow their cars and wind down their windows to banter. I believe a community is safer where its residents, old and young,

A berm can be both a privacy barrier and a showcase for favorite plants. A bare-bones berm was already in place when Marianne Côté-Malley bought half a duplex on a corner lot opposite a school, but she renovated it by removing tired shrubs, bark mulch, and black plastic. She then added new soil and plenty of compost to bring the earth, deadened by the plastic, back to life. She began experimenting with shrubs and perennials, dividing plants frequently to increase the stock. The public side of the berm has more colorful plants – bearded irises, peonies, daylilies, and foxgloves. The inside is viewed close up from a small patio, so Marianne selected plants with a gentler, more muted palette – white Siberian iris, lady's mantle, and spirea – for a more intimate character.

know each other. Talking about gardens and plants is such an easy way to open a friendship.

There are many opportunities for gardening beyond the limits of your own garden. Some gardeners take over adjacent public spaces such as boulevards, road allowances, utility easements, or even traffic islands. These can be very challenging areas to tend; flowers may be picked by schoolchildren for their teachers, the occasional car tire may crush the groundcovers, and litter patrol may become a frequent chore. But the biggest risk is a complaint from a miffed neighbor, so it is wise to involve neighbors in a conservative plan. Save your more inventive gardening ideas for your own land.

In condominium and townhouse complexes, it may be possible to undertake the maintenance of some common areas. If you start small and make everyone welcome in the venture, you have a good chance of getting support for your endeavors from other residents.

Gardening friendships are often a form of partnership. An older couple whose vegetable garden is becoming too large to manage makes new friends by offering growing space to younger gardeners without land of their own. A suburban gardener makes room to overwinter the potted plants of a friend with a balcony garden. (Sinking the pots into the ground prevents damage from rapid freezing and thawing.) It's great fun to do chores in a friend's garden, and to have the favor returned.

Most botanical and public gardens rely on volunteers for a variety of tasks, some involving working with plants, others with people, computers, or books. These positions offer volunteers superb opportunities to extend their horticultural knowledge and meet kindred spirits while supporting the art and science of gardening in the community. Some botanical gardens give extensive training, while at others you'll have on-the-job practice.

As cities grow, allotment gardens are becoming more popular. Typically, these are on publicly owned lands, and are available on a first-come, first-served basis. Water, manure, a compost, benches, and a lockup shed for larger shared tools may be provided, and there may be common areas of fruit trees, beehives, or wild meadows to attract pollinating insects. Allotments were traditionally used for growing fresh vegetables and berries, but flowers, herbs, small trees and shrubs, and impromptu twig sculptures are all found. And because allotment gardens are such pleasant, productive places to see, they are popping up in parks once reserved for lawn.

As in the ancient tradition of the oasis or medieval monastery garden, gardens are protected areas, keeping the outside world at bay, enclosed to foster security and peace. Yet small gardens are like colorful segments in a patchwork quilt. Each is a unique private expression. Combined with other gardens large or small, parks, and street trees, the parts join to take a significant positive role in the environment.

Garden Journeys

I love to visit gardens. Coming to an established garden I've never seen, opening the gate, and entering is always a thrill. Where will the footpaths lead? Toward what will my gaze be directed? Has the space been subdivided? Who is the gardener? What mood has the gardener set? Will there be something unexpected?

Gardens may be limited by site or budget, but gardeners are ingenious at finding ways to work with what they have. After a few years, sometimes sooner, the garden's character begins to emerge. The gardener has learned much about the site, and perhaps has discovered its spirit, its *genius loci.* The space that might have been anything is now something, shaped by trees or shrubs, arbors or borders. Choices have been made, paths forged, structures built, plants selected. Some plants have been moved from spot to spot until they either die or flourish. Design elements, too, may have needed reworking, as the first plan is seldom perfect. Over time, the choices a gardener makes add up to a personal style that might not fit into a category, such as formal or cottage or Japanese or natural, but instead reflect something of the gardener's dreams and intentions. The garden has meaning.

As we keep at this occupation over the years, we grow in as many ways as our plants do. The excitement of learning something new never diminishes, the circle of gardening friends keeps expanding, and somehow the garden becomes a vehicle for creative and spiritual growth.

Many exceptional gardeners do not start to garden in earnest until their

OPPOSITE:
Rosemary and Cliff Bailey made their rambling country garden on a hillside overlooking the dairy farm from which they have retired. The site is open and sunny, with access to plenty of manure. But a garden is more than site and opportunity – it reflects the personality of its makers. Humor and serendipity are apparent throughout, from the wooden crows on the gate to home-built benches, a bumper crop of bird-houses, and a collection of tiny farm implements awaiting grandchildren.

ABOVE:
New leaves of meadow rue (*Thalictrum aquilegiafolium*) unfurl.

Plants may hold special meaning, as does this tree peony (*Paeonia suffruticosa* 'Hawakis'), a gift to Elisabeth and Peter Carey from the clergyman who married them, later given to the author when the Careys moved from their garden.

children are grown or they retire from careers. Others begin as children, helping a parent, grandparent, or neighbor with simple tasks, absorbing without effort plant names and ways of working. My first garden coincided with my first house, and I was wildly enthusiastic, oblivious to my horticultural inexperience. I purchased a few plants that survived, and soon the learning journey began.

Gardeners recognize the need for information and first turn to glossy magazines and brightly illustrated library books. We sign up for courses, attend garden shows, join a botanical garden, a garden club. I remember with gratitude the first course I took years ago, Make a Hanging Moss Basket, given by David Tarrant at the University of British Columbia Botanical Garden, and the relief I felt in acquiring those early skills. Over time, we collect reference books, perhaps subscribe to a specialized journal, write for catalogs, attend a study weekend or an international symposium.

And we find other gardeners with whom to share this spiraling journey. At first, we may ask a more experienced neighbor for a little advice. We ask friends, May I look at your garden? Soon we make new friends just because they garden. We go on organized garden tours, cruise the garden centers and specialty nurseries, visit and revisit botanical gardens, then sign on as volunteers. We may plan vacations abroad that coincide with open gardens or are completely dedicated to garden touring. And the handful of gardening buddies becomes a network, perhaps international, of people who share some of our passion. We may correspond by post, fax, or e-mail, but the reward is the same—we affirm ourselves as gardeners among friends. Gardening in isolation is like cooking for one; it may be satisfactory, but when we reach out and become involved with other gardeners, things really start to cook.

Since gardening is so often private, one of the best things we can do for our gardens is invite others in. For some, this is easy, but for many it feels like a great risk, leaving us vulnerable to the judgment of others. It is a standing joke

The finer points of garden visits

Whether visiting the garden of a friend, going on a self-guided tour of private gardens, or joining an organized bus tour of famous gardens overseas, a little courtesy goes a long way. It is amazing how often gardeners relate the boorish ways visitors have behaved. Here are a few pointers to help secure your welcome.

- Take a genuine interest in the garden. Ask questions. Look carefully. If you're not really interested, stay home.
- Keep to the paths. If you want to see something deep in the border, ask if there is an access path you might use.
- Don't maul the plants, take clippings, steal seeds, or pull labels. Many gardeners will share if you ask. If they won't, assume they have a good reason.
- If you have negative comments to make about a garden, wait until you have left. Gardeners are often very sensitive, and may have excellent hearing.
- Thank the gardener.

that every gardener moans to visitors, "You should have been here two weeks ago." I always tell visitors that my garden is a twenty-year project (this number never lowers) so their expectations will not overwhelm me. Perhaps a sign, Garden Under Renovation, would help. And not all visitors are sympathetic to what you are trying to achieve; some garden clubs are notorious for not paying the slightest attention to a gardener's intentions during private garden tours, pausing only at the pretty plants while ignoring the garden itself. But occasionally one visitor will ask a question or make a remark with the potential to transform the garden. Just as viewing others' gardens can broaden our sense of what a garden might be, the sensitive and astute visitor may help you see your own space with new eyes.

If you discount sore knees, aching shoulders, bad backs, allergic skin rashes, sun wrinkles, freckles, and ugly fingernails, gardening is good for you. The fresh air and exercise keep many people fit, and slow the inevitable aging process. Have you noticed how many older gardeners are able to keep active long after their contemporaries have become sedentary?

Even if gardening is sometimes hard on the body, it is almost always beneficial to the temperament. Far more refreshing than a coffee break are a few moments in the garden to pull weeds or plant a dozen bulbs. A half-day of

Taking care of the gardener

Common sense is easier to give than use, but here are a few nagging reminders to help protect your most valuable gardening tool.

- Protect your skin from accumulated sun exposure with hats and long sleeves. Use sun screen from March to October.
- Stretch back, shoulder, and leg muscles gently before and after gardening sessions. Vary the task frequently so you don't hold one position too long or repeat one action until you ache. Counter muscle effort with frequent mini-stretches.
- Respect your back. Lift with your whole body. Use levers, rollers, and helpers to move anything heavy.
- Spread fall and spring tasks over many months. Chores such as laying mulch, turning over new beds, and moving trees or shrubs can be done on mild days in winter.
- If you just can't keep gloves on, soak your hands before cleaning, scrub with a soft plastic brush, and rub in lots of lotion where the dirt lingers.

A pair of chairs invites lingering in the garden of Shirley Hebenton.

hard pruning is positively therapeutic, unless the results are brutal to the trees and shrubs. If our daily commitments keep us indoors under artificial light and surrounded by synthetic materials, an hour in the garden at the end of each day is an antidote, keeping body rhythms in sync with changing seasonal light and weather. The garden itself is a sanctuary from bustle and stress. It may be the quietest place we have. If we are troubled, gardening is an opportunity to focus attention away from ourselves, a chance to make something positive happen when other areas of life are complicated or overwhelming. If we face serious illness or the loss of someone we love, the garden can contribute greatly to acceptance and healing. As we age, our repeated observations of the life, death, and regeneration of plants help us understand the natural path of our own lives.

Black mondo grass and deer fern carpet part of Jocelyn Horder's garden with dense, handsome foliage.

Victoria gardener Elizabeth England once told how during a bout with cancer she would sit at the bottom of the garden and just stare. Gradually her despair gave way to curiosity about a new shoot emerging or flower bud opening. It gave her the courage to look forward, image a future. When a friend brought an unfamiliar plant, it rekindled in her a sense of purpose beyond illness. Taking part in the tiny miracles of snowdrops or ladybugs or a robin foraging for her family, and witnessing at close hand the grand seasonal cycles, we may absorb some of nature's profound power to heal.

A few hours working in the garden, even a few seconds staring out the window at it, help us temporarily lose the shackles of time. Often I intend to do just one minor chore, spend a few minutes at most, only to find an hour has gone, my clothes need changing, and I have dirt under my fingernails.

The garden is so engaging. We watch carefully as plants perform their varied dances, crocuses pushing the soil aside to make their way, a meadow rue opening its leaves like fingers from a fist, a lily yawning to reveal sensual secrets. The daily progress of a sunflower, twisting from southeast to southwest as it follows the light, is a slow-moving narrative.

At times the garden seems to move too slowly for us. We wait impatiently for the soil to warm up enough for transplanting tender plants, for the trilliums to appear, for the nights to be warm enough to lie out and watch for August's meteors, for plums to ripen, for the magnolia leaves to finish dropping at the end of November. And yet the garden seems to race through its seasons too quickly. The sapling planted the September your son started school has become a towering neighborhood landmark, a worry in a wind storm. Blink, and the snowdrops are gone. The tree peonies are blown. The grasshoppers have arrived. The plums have finished. Summer has flown.

The perception of time is elastic, but gardening allows us to stretch time. Planting is an act of reaching into the future. A carefully chosen tree suitably sited extends our influence well past our own life span. So does participation in the larger gardening fellowship, by planning lasting community projects or by fostering the efforts of younger gardeners. Inevitably we lose some of our finest and most generous gardeners, but they leave us a legacy of shared plants, whole gardens, or the inspiration to become better gardeners.

The garden changes in small ways day by day, year by year, and once in a while by some grand revamping either intentional or through the vagaries of extreme weather, falling trees, or neighborhood construction. We gardeners age too, a little each year, and sometimes find our abilities limited in unexpected ways. Maturing gardeners are faced with fresh challenges, and must outwit their limitations. They begin to look at plants in a new way—How will this perform if I leave it to look after itself? They lose patience with finicky plants that attract aphids or sulk in hot weather. They will not tolerate plants that have let them down. Labor-intensive ones that require deadheading, pruning, or winter protection are replaced by the best of the carefree plants, such as ferns, slow-growing shrubs, and groundcovers. Their

Gardening smarter

Whether limited by time or physical ability, we may come to rely more on experience and knowledge than muscle power. To reduce garden maintenance, avoid some tasks and alter others. Some perennials are just too much work dividing and staking. Give them away.

Lawn maintenance takes too much time to do yourself and too much money to have done. To reduce the lawn area, use alternatives with good form and manageable spread – ferns, ornamental grasses, small rhododendrons, groundcovers. Mulch any open ground to discourage weeds.

Install a sprinkling system to reduce watering and eliminate lugging unwieldy hoses. Get help for heavy work, either a paid gardener or younger gardening friends. Many new gardeners would be delighted to work in exchange for plant divisions.

The best groundcovers are ones that spread to cover the area you want, but are easily controlled so they do not take over the neighborhood. Rate of spread depends not only on the vigor of plants, but also the amount of moisture and light they receive. Here are some groundcovers that are not too finicky about sun or shade.

- *Ajuga reptans* (bugleweed)
- *Arctostaphylos uva-ursi* (bearberry, kinnikinnik)
- *Bergenia* species
- *Dicentra formosa* (native western bleeding heart)
- *Geranium macrorrhizum*
- *Liriope spicata* (lily turf)
- *Lysimachia nummularia* (creeping jenny)
- *Ophiopogon planiscapus* 'Nigrescens' (black mondo grass)
- *Saxifraga* × *urbium* (London pride)
- *Tellima grandiflora* (native fringe-cup)
- *Vinca minor* (periwinkle)
- *Waldsteinia ternata* (barren strawberry)

In late fall, a mature *Enkianthus campanulatus* has turned burnt orange in the garden of Margaret Charlton and Charles Sale. The slow-growing dwarf cypress (*Chamaecyparis pisifera*) is twenty-five years old, but only three feet (one metre) high.

deep knowledge of plants comes not only from reference books or magazines, but from extended experience. There is much to learn from these savvy gardeners who have discovered the most effective ways to cut corners and save effort without compromising their love for a broad spectrum of plants.

The steep woodland garden of Margaret Charlton and Charles Sale has had time to mature gracefully in its quintessentially west coast setting overlooking Burrard Inlet. Mountain ash (*Sorbus* species) and magnolias form an intermediate canopy below the tall second-growth Douglas firs and western hemlocks, a blend of exotic with native plants. Species rhododendrons and other broad-leafed evergreens are reaching their full size, varying from knee-high to huge. Charlie and Margaret have moved some of the largest ones further into the forest to make way for a host of smaller understory plants, especially conifers, that will grow slowly taller and wider, or creep in a prostrate habit. These wise gardeners refuse to baby plants, and those not suited to the high rainfall or summer drought are discarded. They've come to view catalog descriptions such as *dwarf* or *slow-growing* with suspicion; some dwarf trees grow slowly for the first decade, then pick up alarming speed. Gardening is neither static nor permanent, for no amount of maintenance can stop time.

Mature gardens are full of treasures—*Anemone blanda* that have increased in number until they form a magnificent carpet of tiny blooms; perennials in huge drifts or massive clumps, the envy of younger gardeners; flowering shrubs that have grown to elegant proportions; rare trees sprouted from seeds now glorious in their prime. These gardens may have plants that were once nearly impossible to obtain, widely available now because masterful gardeners shared cuttings and seeds with collectors, botanical gardens, and nursery owners so others could grow them. It must amuse them to see how easily we can now buy plants at the garden center that were rare only a decade ago.

Aside from the practical methods and plant information to be gleaned from mature gardeners, there is a contagious optimism that can be felt in their presence. Their excitement about sharing plants and ideas is still fresh, and this keeps the gardening spirit ever young. Hard rains, heavy snow, blistering drought, tomato blight, powdery mildew, changing bylaws, new

The garden mentor

No written description or diagram or even carefully scripted video can match the training of working alongside a good gardener, copying what he or she does. Some experienced gardeners are very generous in helping earnest new gardeners, and may enjoy the role of informal mentor. Taking a hands-on gardening course also builds confidence in working with plants as well as other materials, and what at first seems tricky or mysterious is soon made easy.

Botanical gardens may offer new volunteers training and the chance to work at the elbow of some of the most skilled gardeners in the community. And it is surprising how quickly the uninitiated finds he or she has something to offer in return.

Two exceptional references for locating garden clubs, associations, nurseries, and volunteer opportunities are *The Twelve Month Gardener* (Stevens et al, Whitecap Books, revised 1996) and *The Northwest Gardeners' Resource Directory* (Feeney, Cedarcroft Press, revised 1998).

nomenclature—they've learned to take whatever comes in stride. Next year the weather will be better, the camellias will bloom during a sunny spell, the deer, squirrels, cats, and tent caterpillars will be held at bay, and the sulking clematis will at last surge upward over its intended arch. Hope, optimism, and promise are essential garden elements.

A garden can be a vehicle for creative thinking, even play. Have you never been tempted to fling yourself onto the lawn out of sight of family or public to look about the garden with the eyes of youth, reliving for a few moments the curiosity and openness of your own childhood? Inviting children—your own or someone else's—into the garden can reawaken in you the child's ability to experience the world directly. Discard the plant names and waiting tasks. Look instead at the iridescence of a squirming worm, capture and release a ground beetle, stick your nose so far into a lily that the pollen stains your face.

Imagining is a vital component of garden-making. We gaze out the window at dreary fall downpours, and see drifts of spring bulbs that we intend to plant under the azaleas. We wander around the garden with a black plastic pot, the most recently acquired vine, and envision it scrambling over this arch, through this shrub, along this stretch of fence, before settling on the best spot. Or we stare, over and over, mentally reshaping a bed, building an arbor, installing a pond, revising the curve in a path, getting rid of a hideously overgrown shrub. We garden with our imaginations far more vigorously than with our backs, thereby giving ourselves the pleasure of a thousand different gardens alive within a simple plot. Or we may indulge in a fantasy, perhaps a tropical paradise or an English cottage, then gradually work toward making the garden of the mind a reality.

For gardening to be rewarding, it cannot be merely a set of rules dutifully followed. We may listen to advice about better plants or effective techniques, but only by trial and error do we determine the best ways for ourselves. What seems extravagant, impractical, or foolish can become a stimulating challenge. *Echeveria* can't survive our winters outdoors? Let's try it under a sheet of tempered glass; if it perishes, so be it. Never move a plant in bloom?

Euphorbia amygdaloides 'Rubra' nestles under bronze fennel in the author's garden.

pioneer gardeners

One day I visited Francisca Darts at Dartshill, the Surrey, B.C., garden she and her late husband, Ed, began in 1952. Wide grass paths run through long borders filled with full-grown rhododendrons, towering magnolias, and countless other superb plants. At a crossroads of two paths, Francisca pointed to a clump of *Euphorbia amygdaloides* 'Rubra'. She had brought it home from a visit to Powis Castle in England years before such things could be had easily at a nursery. This particular euphorbia plant, she said, was the source of the ones propagated by a large grower in the Fraser Valley, who had supplied the one now growing in my own garden. The link astounded me. I felt both grateful to Francisca and glad to know a little of our local horticultural heritage.

When VanDusen Botanical Garden was first developed, Ed and Francisca donated dozens of unusual or exotic trees they had grown, many from seed. When the University of British Columbia Botanical Garden expanded into its current site, the Darts were again an invaluable plant source.

Dartshill has been donated to the city of Surrey, and Francisca still works as hard as ever planting new sections, moving large shrubs and small trees to accommodate the greater numbers of visitors who will be able to enjoy this remarkable garden.

Every community has such pioneers, and their stories are the stuff of horticultural legend. Seek them out.

For Victoria gardener Susan Ryley the garden is a work of mutable colors and malleable forms. She is spurred on by a desire for perfection – and at the same time, the need to move on, shift the palette, explore the possibilities, take new risks. She wants to rid the garden of plants that have become clichéd, and to seek more robust colors, more interesting shrubs. Formal elements of the garden plan – clipped hedges, placid lawns, concrete wall and rectangular pond – provide structure that supports her experimentation with unusual plants. Change is at the heart of her garden artistry.

If now is the only chance, we'll just do it, and try to minimize the shock with shade and water. Experimenting is risky, and that sweetens the dividend.

Some gardeners take creative thinking much further, and their gardens become works of art—the land a kind of canvas, the plants and other objects, media manipulated in space and over time. These gardens are rare pleasures, and by visiting them and trying to experience them as fully as possible, using all the senses, we can benefit from the inspirations they afford. It is not so important to copy them, record the names of their plants, or take photos of their clever combinations as it is to seek the passion upon which they are built and to recognize the ways we respond to such gardens emotionally, aesthetically, spiritually.

As a photographer, I often rely on my own garden as a source. It provides specific material for making images, but just as important, it stimulates my creativity. Painters, sculptors, weavers, potters, writers, even dancers and musicians report that their gardens have tangible effects on their work. Sometimes the garden is just a vehicle for getting past creative block, a calming influence in the stormy creative process. At other times the garden plays a more direct role, providing visual and auditory imagery that can be translated into any medium. The vital forces inherent in plants, stone, wood, water are, after all, the very stuff of life, and so provide resonant metaphors of change and cycle, growth and decay, birth and death, isolation and community.

Whether or not you are an artist, your garden puts you in intimate connection with these same forces and metaphors. If while working or resting in the garden you can think clearly, reflect, meditate, you may find yourself open to a spiritual element of the garden which is often felt, but seldom examined or discussed.

We bring to our garden endeavors our own personal histories and cultural

No gardener is too small

The four-year-old neighbor of gardener Nancy Webber asked one summer, "Am I too little to say pelargoniums?" Some families automatically garden together, but neighbors too have a gratifying opportunity to foster the excitement a youngster feels about the plants and animals in the garden. Here are a few of Nancy's child-friendly ways.

- Let children rub the leaves of herbs such as lavender, pineapple sage, or spearmint (it smells just like toothpaste) to release their aromas.
- Grow plants that stimulate the imagination – snapdragons with jaws that open and close, mouse-tail plant (*Arisarum proboscideum*), or anything insectivorous.
- Point out the dewy crystals and diamonds on *Alchemilla mollis* or nasturtium leaves.
- Explain the dangers of eating unknown plants, and the delights of sampling safe ones such as strawberry (*Fragaria* 'Pink Panda'). Many young children like the strong flavors of parsley and chives, and the nectar sucked from petunias, honeysuckle, or nasturtium blossoms.
- Challenge children to find the biggest big-leaf maple leaf in fall.
- Talk about plant names before children are old enough to think they are difficult. Following a treasure hunt is a great way to learn names. ("Look under the hosta behind the rhododendron ...")
- Attract butterflies, birds, and other small animals to the garden by having rough thickets and refusing poisons. Welcome worms rescued from rainy sidewalks.

A handmade wooden gate marks the entrance to Robert Bateman's garden. It includes meaningful details, such as locally hewn posts, an African carving, and carving by a son.

heritage. Since so many of us move, and create one garden after another, the garden is like a photo album, a record that links us to past gardens and garden friends. We try to bring the most important plants with us, the ones with the most meaning, the most potent memories. We collect beach stones, driftwood, mementos—ruins to root the present garden in our associations with other people, places, and times. The details we add to our gardens—things handmade, collected in travels, rescued from the trash, or received as special gifts—may transform the garden, reflecting our personalities, biases, and passions. Even the ashes of loved ones may reside in our gardens, and the markers we make have great significance.

We create a space for ourselves, our families, our special friends. We add a bench for a quiet sit, tables and chairs for sharing convivial meals, decks so we may look out at the world, shelters and bowers in which to hide.

Besides the gardens we actually make, we also carry with us a maze of internal gardens. There are the ones we knew as children, perhaps those of our parents or grandparents. (Whether or not we can actually revisit these gardens, they are germinal.) All our childhood experiences of nature and landscape are lasting sparks for creating our later environments. Gardens and plants are woven through literature, from *Paradise Lost* to *Jack and the Beanstalk*. They have appeared in countless paintings and, more recently, photographs. Some of these images, perhaps the delicately lighted ponds of Monet's Giverny, may also have left impressions. I am certain my love of decaying stumps and mossy places was fostered by the stories of pixies and toadstools told in the Brownie pack and the forest magic affirmed by woodland walks at my grandparents' cottage. Gardens may be powerful places in our dreams and fantasies, even fearsome, entangling jungles in nightmares. No wonder each of us has a different notion of what the garden is. Any of these internal gardens may influence us more than we acknowledge.

For me, the spiritual aspect of gardening is the connection with natural processes. While it is relatively easy in the Pacific Northwest to visit wilderness areas and witness nature on a grand, more-than-human scale, it is not so easy to live in pristine wilderness. But day after day in the garden I have intimate involvement with things that grow and change, die and regenerate. I am as much part of the garden as its location, character, or any of the things in it. Occasionally, when clearing stones, I encounter a salamander, and each time this happens, it takes my breath away. It is a reminder that I am solitary but connected, willful but obedient to the forces and laws of nature.

Each of us makes a garden in our own way, for our own reasons. Is it the garden itself, or the making of it that counts most? Our habits may be delightfully eccentric and our gardens peculiarly eclectic. But we gardeners have much in common, too, and it is worthwhile for us to share with each other more than divisions of favorite plants. Our journeys are highly personal, yet best made in the company of friends.

index

Note that **bold** page numbers indicate photographs.